C·E·L·E·B·R·A·T·I·O·N·S

Also by Diana and Paul von Welanetz:

The Art of Buffet Entertaining
L.A. Cuisine
The Pleasure of Your Company
The von Welanetz Guide to Ethnic Ingredients
With Love from Your Kitchen

C·E·L·E·B·R·A·T·I·O·N·S

A Menu Cookbook
for
Informal Entertaining

Diana and Paul von Welanetz

JEREMY P. TARCHER, Inc.

LOS ANGELES

DISTRIBUTED BY HOUGHTON MIFFLIN COMPANY

BOSTON

Library of Congress Cataloging in Publication Data

Von Welanetz, Diana.
  Celebrations: a menu cookbook for informal entertaining.

  Includes index.
  1. Cookery. 2. Menus. 3. Entertaining.
I. Von Welanetz, Paul. II. Title.
TX715.V787 1985   642'.4   85-4678
ISBN 0-87477-360-1

Copyright © 1985 by Diana and Paul von Welanetz

Jeremy P. Tarcher, Inc.
9110 Sunset Blvd.
Los Angeles, CA 90069

Design by Cynthia Eyring
Illustration by Jennifer Mathews
Photography by Keith Gaynes Photography
Plasticware by Ingrid, Ltd., North Chicago, Illinois
Manufactured in the United States of America
D 10 9 8 7 6 5 4 3 2 1

First Edition

For Pauline, whose inspiration it was. For Lexi who brightens all our days with laughter. For Candace, who lights up our lives with her truth.

CONTENTS

ACKNOWLEDGMENTS

The following people have been helpful in many ways, some with recipes, and some for reminding us to celebrate: Mary Charles, Pat Connell, Pat Crowly, Jennifer Edwards, Jean Hallahan, Janice and Derek Gallagher, Keith Gaynes, Vaughn Greditze, Linda and Ray Hege, Pauline Kelbly, Marion Klaris, Candace Kommers, Steve Koffler, Lana Marder, John and Katie Marin, Joan Nielson, Kay Okrand, Jeanette Marie Paulsen, Robert Rosenberg, Henri Schley, Mimi and Jack Schneider, Tom Sewell, Alice and Fred Simmons, Sandra Stoff, Claudia and Russ Stromberg, Barbara Swain, and Marge Welanetz.

Since what we love has always found

Expression in enduring sound,

Music and verse should be competing

To match the transient joy of eating

There should be present in our songs

As many tastes as there are tongues;

There should be humbly celebrated

One passion that is never sated.

Louis Untermeyer, "Food and Drink"

CELEBRATIONS

THROUGHOUT HISTORY celebrations of all kinds have been synonymous with food—which is an international language, a means of sharing and communication. As food writers, how people gather together to acknowledge the turning of a page of their history has a special fascination for us. Each country has its holiday-related food traditions. In the United States, whose cooks have been exposed to enormous degrees of ethnic influence, it is possible to experience—through food magazines, restaurants, and local food festivals—the culinary traditions of many nations. Sometimes it seems that the food *is* the celebration.

For the two of us, as native East- and West-Coast Americans, holidays have become intermingled with traditional dishes: Thanksgiving turkey with all the trimmings, Christmas roast beef with horseradish and Yorkshire pudding, Easter ham with fresh biscuits, Fourth of July hamburgers and hot dogs with homemade pickles, corn relish, and lemonade. Arm in arm with these traditions go memories of our grandmothers' kitchens, which seemed always to give forth wonderful aromas of coffee, freshly baked breads, cinnamon, and other spices. Generations change, but our mothers found, as their mothers had, that food prepared with love, and shared with treasured friends and family, provided the meeting ground for the best times we remember as families. A favorite food memory was of summertime family-reunion dinner at one uncle's farm, served outdoors on a huge piece of plywood balanced on two sawhorses and covered with oilcloth. The menu was fried chicken, potato salad, Grammy's watermelon pickles, chocolate fudge cake, and homemade ice cream with fresh strawberries.

In this book we share with you menus we have served at our own celebrations. We look at nature as a playground, exploring the possibilities of dining in easy intimacy with the outdoors. The menus are not representative of any particular style of cooking, but have a somewhat traditional flavor that just seems comfortable.

S PRING

S PRING is the time of new beginning. We feel a quickening, an anticipation of longer, gentler days and deeper blue skies. There is still a nip in the air, but we begin to think about venturing outdoors. Our first picnic of the season will be designed around a bicycle excursion we've been planning for the first warm day.

The spring holidays of Easter and Passover, May Day, Mother's Day, and June Weddings are fast approaching. Fresh young greens begin appearing in the produce section of the market and we welcome simpler, lighter, meals that incorporate them. The first asparagus of the season inspires us to create a luncheon to celebrate Easter, using it as a salad course. Who can every have too much of the first asparagus?

Now it's time to plant the herb garden that will provide us with its aromatic bounty through the summer, and to set out different types of tomato plants, some early-bearing and some late. We replant all the planters, buy new outdoor cushions, sand and repaint the garden furniture. With everything looking so bright and new, we'll invite friends in to see our garden and enjoy a brunch menu that is very easy on the hosts.

The approach of spring also makes us think about our bodies, which have been neglected a bit during the winter, and start getting in shape for the summer. With this concentration on fitness, we think of light and simple foods to enjoy in new ways. Our recent passion for sushi inspires an ideal menu to serve after a dip in an Oriental hot tub or anywhere we might find a Japanese garden.

As we said, this is the time of new beginnings, and spring would not be spring without at least one wedding to celebrate. So our fantasy wedding menu features a delicious salad made with fresh spring artichoke hearts, and a cake decorated with the first berries of the year.

A BICYCLE BASKET PICNIC
(FOR 2)

Zinfandel

Apple with Core of Roquefort

Pita Pockets with Three Fillings:
Ratatouille Niçoise
Bulgur Salad (Tabouli)
Cream Cheese and Madeira-Soaked Raisins

Lazy Almond Macaroons

A BICYCLE BASKET PICNIC

Always hurrying from place to place, crowding the legal speed limit, we acquire a lopsided perspective of the world we live in. To rediscover the rhythms of earth and nature try a bicycle picnic just for the two of you. Aside from being good for your body, it is healing to your being. At five miles per hour you become aware of the sounds around you: neighborhood piano lessons, angry sparrows scolding thieving crows, the sound of rustling bushes, the sweet smell of spring blossoms, the fresh ocean air or a warm, earthy breeze. By late March we feel a compelling need to oil up our bikes and get out into the world to investigate all this firsthand.

For our first outing we pedal only about five miles south to a marina, where we picnic on the side of an inlet and watch the sailboats tack in and out of the harbor. We sit sometimes on the large brown rocks edging the waterway, or on the grass further inland near a bird sanctuary, and slowly enjoy a fresh, light lunch as as we watch the parade of spanking white sails and seagulls.

Since both space and weight can be challenges on a bicycle, we've brought a folded sheet rather than a blanket. And once that is comfortably arranged we can begin in earnest to explore the contents of our picnic container. First to appear is a small round tray with two wine glasses, followed by three bowls and three serving spoons, one containing ratatouille, another, a bulgur wheat salad flecked with parsley, and a third with cream cheese and raisins. Then come two dishes with three half slices of round pita bread each, which, if carefully separated, become hollow pockets for the fillings. Lunch begins, though, with a red apple which has simply been cored and stuffed with Roquefort cheese. Each quarter-inch slice of tangy apple contains an aromatic round core of cheese.

Ah, the simple life; but this is not all. We often linger on the grass in the warm afternoon sun in no hurry to hurry. And this requires nourishment, supplied by wholesome and chewy almond macaroons.

Since lunch was satisfying yet light, pedaling home should be easy and pleasant.

SHOPPING LIST

- 1 small onion (½ cup minced)
- 1 small eggplant
- 1 small zucchini
- 1 small red or green bell pepper
- 1 cucumber (preferably hothouse type)
- 5 medium-size ripe tomatoes (preferably plum)
- 1 bunch scallions
- Fresh parsley
- Fresh basil (2 teaspoons chopped)
- Fresh oregano (1½ teaspoons chopped)
- Fresh mint (2 tablespoons chopped)
- 1 head romaine lettuce
- 2 red Delicious apples
- 1 lemon (for juice)
- 11 ounces cream cheese
- 3 ounces Roquefort or other blue-veined cheese
- 1 package pita bread
- 1 cup bulgur wheat
- 7 ounce package almond paste
- 1 tablespoon raisins, dried currants, or dates
- 1 bottle (750 ml) Zinfandel
- About 2 tablespoons dry Sherry or Madeira

Staples

- Olive oil (about ½ cup)
- 1 egg white
- 1 garlic clove
- ¾ cup sugar
- 2 teaspoons raw sugar (turbinado)
- 1 teaspoon Amaretto liqueur (optional)
- Worcestershire sauce (½ teaspoon)
- Dried basil (½ teaspoon, if fresh is not available)
- Dried oregano (½ teaspoon, if fresh is not available)
- Ground turmeric (¼ teaspoon), optional
- Cinnamon or allspice (½ teaspoon)
- Salt
- Black pepper

DO-AHEAD TIMETABLE

Up to a month ahead: Make cookies and freeze

Up to five days ahead: Make Ratatouille Niçoise, Bulgur Salad, and Cream Cheese fillings

One day ahead: Prepare apples with Roquefort. Pack all nonperishables in basket or hamper

Just before leaving for picnic: Pack cold items

A Bicycle Basket Picnic

 ## Apple with Core of Roquefort

FOR 2 SERVINGS

2 red Delicious, McIntosh, *or* other red apples of your choice
2 to 3 ounces Roquefort *or* other blue-veined cheese

Use an apple corer to remove the cores from the apples. Fill the resulting holes with cheese, packing it in firmly. Chill. Slice the apple with a very thin slicing knife into ¼-inch horizontal slices, but leave the slices in place and the apple in its original shape.

To eat, separate the slices one at a time.

To Prepare in Advance: Wrap tightly in plastic and wrap again in foil. Chill for up to 2 days.

 ## Pita Pockets with Three Fillings

FOR 2 SERVINGS

Pita bread (pocket bread, *khubz, eish shami,* or Arab or Syrian bread) is available in supermarkets, Middle Eastern bakeries, and natural food stores across the country, thanks to America's abounding interest in ethnic cuisines. You will find it made with white flour, wholewheat flour, and even bran, sometimes sprinkled with sesame seed. A natural pocket forms in the bread during baking, which makes it ideal for stuffing with all kinds of salads and sandwich fillings. You may wish to have a simple, impromptu picnic with traditional sandwich meats, cheeses, and spreads, or to be more elaborate and supply one or more of the following fillings. Any leftover fillings will keep in the refrigerator for up to 5 days.

3 whole pitas (whatever variety you choose), halved crosswise

At the picnic site, fill the 6 pita pockets with the following fillings:

Ratatouille

MAKES ABOUT 3 CUPS

Ratatouille is a French country specialty that can be served warm or cold, as an appetizer spread, a vegetable dish, and even an omelet filling. It just seems to *belong* on a picnic.

½ cup minced onion
3 tablespoons olive oil
1 garlic clove, chopped
1 small eggplant, cut into ½-inch dice
1 small zucchini, halved lengthwise, then cut into ¼-inch slices
1 small red or green bell pepper, seeds and membranes removed, cut in ½-inch dice
3 medium-size ripe tomatoes (preferably plum), halved, seeded, and diced (do not peel)
1 tablespoon minced fresh parsley
2 teaspoons fresh basil, finely chopped, *or* ½ teaspoon dried basil, crumbled
1½ teaspoons fresh oregano, chopped, *or* ½ teaspoon dried oregano, crumbled
½ teaspoon salt
¼ teaspoon freshly ground black pepper

Sauté the onion in the olive oil in a medium skillet (preferably nonstick) until transparent but not browned. Add the garlic and sauté briefly. Add the eggplant, zucchini, and bell pepper. Cover and cook over medium heat for 10 minutes. Uncover, add the remaining ingredients, and cook over medium-high heat until the mixture is thickened and most of the liquid given off by the vegetables has evaporated. Cool at least an hour before serving to allow flavors to blend.

To Prepare in Advance: Store, covered, in the refrigerator for up to 5 days.

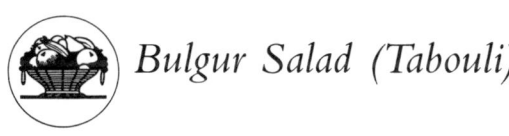 *Bulgur Salad (Tabouli)*

MAKES ABOUT 3 CUPS

Tabouli, a popular Middle Eastern salad flavored with olive oil, lemon, and parsley, is easy to make and requires no cooking.

1   cup bulgur wheat (see Note 1)
2   cups boiling water or clear chicken broth
½   medium cucumber, peeled, seeded, and diced
4   scallions (including part of the green tops), sliced
½   cup minced fresh parsley
2   tablespoons or more chopped fresh mint
2   medium-size ripe tomatoes, halved, seeded, and diced (do not peel), or 3 to 4 sun-dried tomatoes (see Note 2)
   Leaves from the center of a head of romaine lettuce

DRESSING:

⅓   cup olive oil
3   tablespoons fresh lemon juice
1   teaspoon salt
   Freshly ground black pepper to taste
¼   teaspoon ground cinnamon or allspice (optional)

Note 1: Bulgur is made by crushing wheat berries that have first been steamed and dried. The medium grind is sold in many supermarkets and health food stores. Cracked wheat, which is not steamed before crushing, may be substituted. The fine or medium grinds of either product are ideal for recipes that require only that the wheat be soaked.

Note 2: Sun-dried tomatoes, packed in olive oil and sometimes flavored with garlic and herbs, are available in jars in gourmet specialty stores. They are expensive, but a little goes a long way to lend a piquant flavor to many salads and pasta dishes. For a less traditional tabouli, use some of the tangy oil from the tomato jar in place of a small part of the oil in the dressing.

Place the bulgur in a mixing bowl and pour the boiling water or chicken broth over it. Let stand for 30 to 45 minutes, or until softened. Shake the mixture dry in a strainer and return to the bowl. Add remaining salad ingredients except tomatoes and romaine.

To make the dressing, whisk together the dressing ingredients. Pour over the soaked wheat mixture and toss lightly. Fold in the chopped tomatoes.

To fill pita pockets, line each first with small leaves of romaine lettuce.

To Prepare in Advance: Store tabouli in a covered non-metal container in the refrigerator for up to 5 days.

 ## Cream Cheese and Madeira-Soaked Raisins

MAKES ABOUT 1½ CUPS

We keep in our refrigerator a small container of raisins or dried currants covered with Madeira or Sherry. They make a flavorful addition to many spreads, salads, and sauces.

- 1 tablespoon raisins, dried currants, *or* finely chopped dates
  Dry Sherry or Madeira
- 11 ounces cream cheese, at room temperature
- ¼ teaspoon turmeric, for a golden color (optional)

Soak raisins or currants in boiling water for 10 minutes and drain well. Cover with Sherry or Madeira. Let stand at least 30 minutes, or indefinitely in the refrigerator. (If using dates, do not soak; add Sherry or Madeira directly to cream cheese mixture.) Mix all ingredients and chill.

To Prepare in Advance: Store in the refrigerator for up to 5 days.

Lazy Almond Macaroons

MAKES ABOUT 18 COOKIES

1 package (7 ounces) almond paste (should feel soft)
¾ cup sugar
1 egg white
1 teaspoon Amaretto liqueur (optional)
2 teaspoons raw sugar (turbinado sugar)

Cut almond paste into pieces and place in bowl of an electric mixer with the sugar. Beat until crumbly. Add the egg white and optional liqueur and beat until smooth.

Drop by teaspoonfuls onto a greased and floured baking sheet, leaving at least an inch between the cookies. Smooth tops with dampened fingers. Sprinkle the raw sugar over the macaroons and let stand, uncovered, at room temperature for 3 hours.

Preheat oven to 325° and place rack in center position. Bake for 20 to 30 minutes until dry to the touch and golden brown. Remove from oven and loosen with spatula; finish cooling on a rack.

To Prepare in Advance: Store in an airtight container between layers of waxed paper in a cool place for up to a week, or store in freezer indefinitely.

A CELEBRATION OF SPRING EASTER LUNCHEON
(FOR 12)

Children: Lemonade

Adults: Iced tea

Dry Rosé or Champagne

Torta d'Alba

Platter of Asparagus Vinaigrette

Amaretto Fudge Cake

Garnished with Fresh Violets

Basket of Fresh Strawberries with
Whipped Cream and Brown Sugar for Dipping

A CELEBRATION OF SPRING EASTER LUNCHEON

In late March or April, when the buds are first beginning to show green on our sycamore tree, we begin to give more attention to the weather and try to guess what it will be like on Easter. Soon there will be an egg hunt to plan—a good excuse for a gathering of friends and family. Everyone delights in the newness and the fresh exhilaration of spring, as if each had some secret reason for finally and officially putting an end to winter.

There is always the possibility that undependable weather may dampen some of the fun of this first outdoor party of the year, so we advise that you "escape" only as far away as your patio. The weather may turn out to be perfect, but if it's tricky and contrary, a quick organization of forces can simply and easily move your festivities under cover.

We plan a menu that will be flexible enough to serve whether children are present or not. Lemonade is the perfect outdoor Easter drink for youngsters, and iced tea will do nicely for the adults.

Our Torta d'Alba fits this occasion wonderfully. It is robustly satisfying, with its rich, golden brown crust enclosing moist layers of pimiento, ham, spinach, and omelet. It is complemented by a simple salad of asparagus spears, shiny in a light wash of vinaigrette dressing.

The grand finale, Amaretto Fudge Cake garnished with fresh violets, is designed especially for the adults. The children will probably prefer luscious fresh strawberries, dipped into whipped cream and dusted with brown sugar.

You'll find this menu wonderfully adaptable not only for Easter luncheon, but at any time of the day or year. However, the lovely asparagus salad must wait for whenever asparagus is plentiful.

SHOPPING LIST

- 4 pounds fresh asparagus
- 3 or 4 baskets strawberries
- 8 ounces mushrooms
- 8 ounces red bell peppers or 16 ounces canned whole pimientos
- Scallions (¼ cup minced)
- 1 small bunch fresh chives
- Lemons (for lemonade)
- Fresh parsley (2 teaspoons minced
- 1 lemon (for juice)
- 8 ounces thinly sliced prosciutto or 12 ounces sliced baked ham
- 12 ounces sliced Swiss cheese
- Parmesan cheese (for ¼ cup grated)
- 2 cups (16 ounces) heavy cream
- Eggs (3 dozen)
- ½ stick butter
- 2½ sticks unsalted butter
- ¼ cup cream, half and half, or milk
- 3 packages (10 ounces each) frozen chopped spinach
- 2 pounds fresh or frozen puff pastry or 3 packages (10 ounces each) frozen patty shells
- Tea
- 6 ounces unsweetened chocolate
- ½ box light brown sugar
- About 24 to 36 whole almonds
- 4 bottles (750 ml) dry rosé or champagne (optional)
- 6 tablespoons Amaretto liqueur

Staples

- Garlic (½ teaspoon minced)
- Olive oil (6 tablespoons)
- Red wine vinegar (2 tablespoons)
- Dijon mustard (1 tablespoon)
- All-purpose flour (1¼ cups)
- Sugar (2½ cups)
- Powdered sugar (½ cup)
- *Herbes de Provence*, Italian herb seasoning, or other herb blend (½ teaspoon)
- Salt
- Black pepper
- Cayenne pepper
- Whole nutmeg (for ¼ teaspoon freshly grated)
- Worcestershire sauce (¾ teaspoon)
- Vanilla (2 teaspoons)

From a variety store

- Fruitcake tin (10 inches in diameter)
- 1½ yards lilac grosgrain ribbon
- Rubber bands (6 to 8)

From a nursery or flower shop

- 8 or more African violet blossoms (or other nontoxic flowers)

DO-AHEAD TIMETABLE

Up to a month ahead: Bake and freeze the Amaretto Fudge Cake

Up to a week ahead: Make vinaigrette

Up to three days ahead: Bake the Torta d'Alba

One day ahead: Prepare asparagus platter

Day of the party: Make lemonade and iced tea. Glaze cake and decorate with violets. Whip cream

Just before the party: Rinse and dry strawberries

 *Torta d'Alba*

FOR 8 TO 12 SERVINGS (MAKE TWO IF APPETITES ARE HEARTY)

A multi-layered feast appropriate for just about any indoor or outdoor adventure, at any time of day. It is very easy to make, in spite of the lengthy directions. You will need a 10-inch by 3-inch round springform pan to make this. *Duxelles* is a mixture of minced cooked mushrooms used to flavor sauces, egg dishes, and as a stuffing in French cooking. We keep it on hand in the freezer and use it here as one of the flavorful layers.

2 pounds fresh or frozen puff pastry *or* 3 packages (10 ounces each) frozen patty shells, thawed
2 eggs
¼ cup freshly grated Parmesan cheese
12 ounces Swiss cheese, sliced
8 ounces thinly sliced prosciutto *or* 12 ounces sliced baked ham
8 ounces fresh red bell peppers, roasted and skinned (see Note) *or* 16 ounces canned whole pimientos, opened flat, rinsed, and drained

SPINACH LAYER:

3 packages (10 ounces each) frozen chopped spinach, thawed
     and squeezed of all moisture
½ teaspoon salt
¼ teaspoon freshly ground black pepper
¼ teaspoon freshly grated nutmeg

DUXELLES:

8 ounces fresh mushrooms
2 tablespoons (¼ stick) butter
¼ cup minced scallions
½ teaspoon minced garlic
2 teaspoons fresh lemon juice
¼ teaspoon salt
   Pinch of cayenne pepper

EGG LAYER:

2 tablespoons (¼ stick) butter
½ teaspoon *Herbes de Provence,* Italian herb seasoning, *or* other
     herb blend
12 eggs
¼ cup cream, half and half, or milk
½ teaspoon salt

Note: Roast peppers directly over a medium-high gas flame on the stove (or broil 1 inch from the heat if you have an electric range). Use tongs to turn the peppers so the skin turns black and blisters all over. Place in a plastic bag and set aside for 5 to 10 minutes. Remove from bag, cut in half lengthwise and remove the seeds and membranes. Rinse off the charred skin under cold running water, or use the dull edge of a chef's knife to scrape away the skin. Blot dry.

To make the bottom crust, stack 13 of the patty shells (or 1½ pounds puff pastry) on a lightly floured surface and press down firmly with your hands to form one large patty. Flour the top and bottom of the pastry well and roll out to a large circle measuring 17 inches in diameter. Wrap the dough around the rolling pin and lift it over the pan, easing it in gently. Press the dough against the bottom and sides, leaving a ½-inch overhang. Separate one egg and lightly beat the white; reserve the yolk for the egg layer. With a pastry brush cover the entire inside surface of the pastry, including the overhang, with the beaten white (this will "waterproof" the pastry and prevent it from becoming soggy when the filling is added). Refrigerate until needed.

Preheat the oven to 425°F. To assemble the torta, evenly sprinkle the bottom of the prepared shell with half the Parmesan. Top with a layer of half the Swiss cheese and half the prosciutto.

To make the spinach layer, mix the spinach with the salt, pepper, and nutmeg. Distribute it evenly over the prosciutto. Top with the red peppers or pimientos.

To make the duxelles, chop the mushrooms very finely by hand or in a food processor. Sauté them in the butter with the scallions and garlic in a 9- to 10-inch skillet (preferably nonstick) over medium-high heat until they have released all of their moisture and are very dry. Season to taste with lemon juice, salt, and a sprinkling of cayenne. Spread the mushroom mixture over the pimientos in the crust.

To make the egg layer, melt the butter with the dried herbs over medium-high heat in the pan in which the mushrooms were cooked; it is not necessary to rinse it. Whisk the eggs with the reserved yolk and cream until thoroughly blended. Pour the mixture into the sizzling herb butter. Cook until set but still soft and creamy, like scrambled eggs. Turn out of the pan to make a layer over the mushrooms. Top with the remaining ham or prosciutto followed by the remaining Swiss and Parmesan.

To make the top crust, stack the remaining 5 patty shells (or ½ pound puff pastry) on a lightly floured surface and shape into a large patty. Flour the top and bottom well and roll into a circle 11 inches in diameter. Ease the crust over the filling. Fold the edges of the lower crust with the top crust to form an even roll around the inside rim of the pan. Crimp the rim decoratively as desired. Beat the remaining egg and brush over the entire top surface of the torta to turn it golden as it bakes. With a thin, sharp knife, make several small cuts in the top pastry for steam vents. Place the pan on a baking sheet with a rim, which will catch any butter that may leak out during baking. Do not hold the torta at this point, as it contains warm layers of food and must be cooked to eliminate the possibility of spoilage.

Bake for 10 minutes, then lower the heat to 400°F and continue baking for 45 minutes longer or until the top is golden brown. Cool on a rack for at least

30 minutes before removing the side of the springform.

The best way to slice the torta into wedges is with an electric carving knife or a serrated knife, so the layers won't be crushed from too much pressure.

Serve warm or at room temperature.

To Prepare in Advance: Once baked and cooled, the torta may be stored in the refrigerator up to 3 days (the egg layer does not freeze well). The duxelles may be stored a week or longer in the refrigerator in a non-metal container, or up to 6 months in the freezer.

 *Platter of Asparagus Vinaigrette*

FOR 12 SERVINGS

Asparagus is in season during March, April, and May. Celebrate its appearance with this special salad. Because of the quantity involved, we recommend a brief boiling, rather than steaming, which is the method we prefer for smaller amounts.

> 4 pounds fresh asparagus
> Salt
> 6 to 8 hard-cooked eggs, finely chopped
> 1 small bunch fresh chives, snipped
>
> MUSTARD VINAIGRETTE:
> 2 tablespoons fresh lemon juice
> 1 tablespoon Dijon mustard
> 6 tablespoons olive oil
> 2 teaspoons minced fresh parsley
> Salt and freshly ground black pepper to taste
> 2 egg whites, beaten until frothy

Peel the stalks of the asparagus with a vegetable peeler to remove any woody exterior. Fill a large roasting pan about ¾ full of water and add approximately 1 teaspoon salt per quart. Bring to a rapid boil. Drop in the asparagus spears and bring quickly back to a boil. Simmer for 3 to 4 minutes, or until a knife inserted in the lower stalk of the asparagus slips in easily. Drain and immediately pour cold water over the asparagus to cool it, then drain again and dry on towels.

To make the vinaigrette, combine all ingredients except egg whites. Fold in the egg whites, which will make the dressing cling to the asparagus. Refrigerate for at least 1 hour or up to 24 hours.

To serve, arrange the asparagus on a serving platter. Combine the hard-cooked eggs with the minced chives. Sprinkle a band of chopped egg down the center of the asparagus.

To Prepare in Advance: Prepare the asparagus no sooner than the night before your party, or it will lose its crisp quality and bright color. The mustard vinaigrette, except for the addition of egg whites, keeps for a week in the refrigerator.

Amaretto Fudge Cake Garnished with Fresh Violets

FOR 12 TO 16 SERVINGS

The center of this cake should be soft and fudgy, like a gooey brownie. The double chocolate glaze hardens to a smooth, lustrous sheen, capturing a few petals of fresh violets or other nontoxic flowers that decorate the top.

CAKE:

	Shortening to grease pan
5	ounces unsweetened chocolate
1¼	cups (2½ sticks) unsalted butter
5	eggs
2½	cups sugar
1¼	cups all-purpose flour
2	tablespoons Amaretto liqueur
1½	teaspoons vanilla
¼	teaspoon salt
⅓	cup chopped toasted almonds
1 to 2	tablespoons Amaretto, to sprinkle over the warm cake

GLAZE:

2 bars (3 ounces each) Lindt Excellence or Tobler Tradition
    bittersweet chocolate
1 ounce unsweetened chocolate
3 tablespoons water
3 tablespoons unsalted butter, cut into small pieces
2 tablespoons Amaretto
⅓ cup chopped almonds

TO DECORATE:

24 to 36 whole blanched toasted almonds
    Fresh African violet blossoms or other nontoxic flowers
    (see Note)

Note: You may wish to use candied violets, available at gourmet specialty stores, rather than fresh violets.

Preheat the oven to 350°F. Grease a 9-inch round springform pan or deep layer cake pan with shortening. Cut a circle of foil or parchment paper to fit the bottom of the pan; grease the paper.

To make the cake, melt the chocolate with the butter over low heat in a heavy-bottomed saucepan, taking care not to scorch it. Set aside to cool.

Combine eggs and sugar in a large mixing bowl and whisk just until blended and smooth; do not overbeat. Stir in the chocolate mixture. Add the flour, amaretto, vanilla, and salt and mix just until blended. Fold in the chopped almonds.

Place the prepared pan on a heavy baking sheet for ease of handling. Pour in the batter. Bake for 60 to 75 minutes, or until the center is firm to the touch. Cool in the pan for 15 minutes, then invert onto a rack to cool, removing the foil or parchment. Sprinkle while still warm with 1 to 2 tablespoons amaretto. Cool completely before glazing.

To make the glaze, melt the two chocolates with the water in a very heavy saucepan over low heat. When smooth, mix in the pieces of butter until melted, then remove from the heat. Stir in the amaretto. Leave at room temperature for up to 2 hours before glazing the cooled cake.

When ready to glaze the cake, place it upside down on a piece of waxed paper, which will catch any drips. Set the pan of glaze in a large pan of ice water and beat by hand until the glaze is just thick enough to spread. Remove the pan from the ice water and pour the glaze over the top of the cake. Spread it evenly over the top and sides, smoothing it with a spatula.

Before the glaze has hardened, press toasted almonds about an inch apart in a circle around the top of the cake near the edge, pointed ends down. If desired, make another circle of almonds about an inch closer to the center. Place violets (or other flowers) in the center.

This dessert is very rich, so we recommend cutting it into thin slices. Serve sweetened whipped cream flavored with Amaretto as an accompaniment.

To Prepare in Advance: The cake may be glazed up to 24 hours before serving. Store, covered, at room temperature. Freezing changes the appearance of the glaze, but the unglazed cake freezes for up to 3 months.

Basket of Fresh Strawberries with Whipped Cream and Brown Sugar for Dipping

FOR 12 SERVINGS

3 or 4	baskets fresh strawberries, preferably with stems
2	cups heavy cream (whipping cream)
⅓ to ½	cup powdered sugar, sifted
2	teaspoons vanilla
½	*freshly opened* 1-pound box light brown sugar (do not pack)

Do not rinse the berries when you bring them home from the market. They should be rinsed only briefly just before serving.

Combine the cream, powdered sugar, and vanilla in a large *chilled* electric mixer bowl. Whip until it holds soft peaks. Transfer to a serving bowl and chill.

As close as possible to serving time, rinse the berries briefly under cold water and blot dry; do not hull. Arrange in an attractive basket (we use a heart-shaped wicker basket) or other serving container. Set on a dessert table with the whipped cream and brown sugar for dipping. Guests pick up the berries by stem or hull, dip in cream, and then in sugar.

To Prepare in Advance: Whip the cream up to 8 hours before serving and chill in its serving bowl.

A KITCHEN BRUNCH BUFFET
(FOR 20)

Mimosas or Fresh Orange Juice

Mini-Bagels with Smoked Salmon Spread and Dill

Egg Casserole Chimay

Basket of Skewered Fruits

Frances's Fudge Muffins
or
Assorted Croissants

Coffee

A Kitchen Brunch Buffet

Brunch is late breakfast, early lunch, or a combination of the two. It can be one of the easiest and most enjoyable meals to share with guests because everyone feels fresh and relaxed so early in the day. Much of the preparation can be done the evening before—the table set, the coffee ready to perk. And brunch is simple, with no dessert required.

To celebrate the arrival of spring, decorate the kitchen counter where the buffet will be served with small herb plants, perhaps to be replanted later in the garden.

Begin by offering each arriving guest either a steaming mug of coffee or a Mimosa, a bubbling Champagne and fresh orange juice combination. Guests serve themselves from a buffet that features tiny bagels topped with smoked salmon spread and fresh dill sprigs. The main attraction, a real winner, is a puffy egg and mushroom casserole based on the flavors of the classic French *Oeufs à la Chimay*. On a flat basket covered with nontoxic leaves arrange skewers of the choicest available spring fruit. Steaming hot Fudge Muffins that you make that morning can be served in a napkin-lined basket, or make it very easy on yourself by purchasing assorted flavors of flaky freshly baked croissants from a local bakery.

SHOPPING LIST

- 4 quarts fresh orange juice
- 2 pounds mushrooms
- 1 bunch scallions

  Shallots (⅓ cup chopped) or an additional bunch of scallions

  Fresh dill
- 2 Italian plum tomatoes or 1 basket cherry tomatoes
- 2 baskets strawberries
- ½ honeydew melon
- 1 cantaloupe
- ½ pineapple
- ¼ watermelon
- 1 lemon (for juice)
- 8 ounces smoked salmon
- 1 pound Swiss cheese

  Parmesan cheese (for ⅓ cup grated)
- 1 pound cream cheese
- 2 dozen eggs
- 7 sticks butter
- 2 quarts half and half or light cream
- 1 cup (8 ounces) heavy cream

  Paper liners for muffin tins
- 4 cups chopped walnuts
- 2 bars (4 ounces each) sweet chocolate

  Package of bamboo skewers (6 to 8 inches long)
- 36 croissants (if not serving muffins)
- 24 mini-bagels (if not available, use 12 regular bagels)
- 6 bottles Champagne

  Ice to chill bottles of Champagne and orange juice

Staples

- Sugar (3¼ cups)
- All-purpose flour (4¼ cups)
- Coffee
- Cocoa (2 tablespoons)
- Whole nutmeg (for ¼ teaspoon freshly grated)
- Vanilla (2 teaspoons)
- Salt
- Black pepper
- White pepper

From the garden, nursery, or florist

- Spring flowers such as tulips or daffodils
- About 20 large leaves (such as ivy, citrus, or camellia)

DO-AHEAD TIMETABLE

Up to a month ahead: Make and freeze muffins

Up to a week ahead: Make salmon spread

One day ahead: Prepare egg casserole for baking; refrigerate. Thaw muffins

Day of the party: Skewer fruit

Just before the party: Ice the bottles of Champagne and orange juice. Spread
 bagels with salmon spread and garnish with dill. Bake casserole

During the party: Heat croissants or muffins. Keep casserole warm on hot
 tray

Mimosas

FOR 20 SERVINGS

Some of your guests may prefer plain freshly squeezed orange juice, but the
addition of Champagne (or sparkling white wine, as it must be called if produced
outside the Champagne region of France), transforms the juice into a festive
morning drink.

    4   quarts fresh orange juice
5 to 6 bottles Champagne or other sparkling white wine

Place bottles of juice and Champagne in the sink and bury them in a blanket
of ice. Guests mix their own drinks to taste.

Mini-Bagels with Smoked Salmon Spread and Dill

MAKES 48 INDIVIDUAL PIECES

If you can't find mini-bagels, halve large bagels horizontally, then cut them
into bite-size pieces. Serve the spread in a crock as a sort of pâté, garnished with
tomato and dill.

    1   pound cream cheese, softened
    6   scallions, sliced
    8   ounces smoked salmon

25

TO GARNISH AND SERVE:

24 mini-bagels, halved and toasted, *or* 4 large bagels, prepared according to above directions

2 Italian plum tomatoes, quartered lengthwise and sliced, *or* 16 cherry tomatoes, cut into wedges

Sprigs of fresh dill

Place the cream cheese in a food processor or blender and process until creamy, then add scallions and salmon. Process until thoroughly blended, stopping the motor once or twice to scrape down the sides of the container with a rubber spatula.

Spread the mixture on toasted bagels. Garnish each serving with a quarter slice of tomato or wedge of cherry tomato and a sprig of fresh dill.

To Prepare in Advance: Store the spread in the refrigerator up to a week. Spread on bagels and garnish within an hour of serving.

Egg Casserole Chimay

FOR 20 TO 24 SERVINGS

This is a delicious and easy dish to serve a large group. It is based on a recipe given to us years ago by our friend Flo Braker. The egg mixture puffs dramatically, doubling in height. After some improvising in the kitchen we have also served this with a filling of green chiles and one of Italian sausages in a tomato and green pepper sauce, both with great success.

Butter to grease baking dish

CHEESE-EGG LAYER:

1 cup (2 sticks) butter or margarine
2 cups all-purpose flour (instant-blending flour is good here)
2 quarts half and half or light cream
16 eggs, beaten
1 pound Swiss cheese, shredded

2   teaspoons salt
¼   teaspoon freshly ground black pepper
¼   teaspoon freshly grated nutmeg

MUSHROOM FILLING:

2   pounds mushrooms, finely chopped
½   cup (1 stick) butter
⅓   cup minced shallots *or* the white part of scallions, thinly sliced
¼   cup all-purpose flour (instant-blending preferred)
1   cup heavy cream
1   teaspoon fresh lemon juice
    Salt and freshly ground white pepper to taste
⅓   cup grated Parmesan cheese

Preheat the oven to 400°F and set the rack in the upper third of the oven. Butter two 13x9x2-inch baking dishes (or one large baking dish of 18 to 20 cups capacity).

To make the cheese-egg mixture which will form two of the layers, melt 1 cup butter in a large skillet. Stir in the flour and cook for 3 to 4 minutes, stirring often. Remove from heat and whisk in the half and half. Return the pan to medium heat and cook, whisking often, until thickened. Stir in the cheese, salt, pepper, and nutmeg. Remove from heat. Whisk in beaten eggs until well combined.

To make the mushroom filling, sauté the mushrooms and shallots in butter in a large skillet over medium-high heat for 5 minutes. Sprinkle with the flour and stir to coat the mushrooms. Pour in the cream and cook over medium heat, stirring often, until thickened. Stir in lemon juice. Season to taste with salt and pepper.

To assemble the casserole, pour half the cheese-egg mixture into the bottom of the prepared baking dish(es), smoothing it to make an even layer. Spread the mushroom filling evenly over the top. Cover with the remaining egg mixture. Sprinkle with grated Parmesan cheese.

Bake for 45 minutes, or until puffed and lightly browned. Serve at once, placing the casserole on a warming tray if it is to be left standing longer than 20 minutes.

To Prepare in Advance: After assembling the casserole in the baking dish(es), cover and refrigerate. Bake the chilled casserole for 50 to 55 minutes.

 *Basket of Skewered Fruits*

FOR 20 SERVINGS

An easy and beautiful way to serve fresh fruit with any buffet menu. Include berries that are just appearing in the markets.

  20 bamboo skewers, 6 to 8 inches long
        A basket or serving dish lined with washed nontoxic leaves such as ivy or citrus leaves
        Fresh spring flowers, such as tulips or daffodils, to decorate
  20 large strawberries
  ½ honeydew melon, peeled, seeded, and cut into bite-size cubes
  ½ fresh pineapple, peeled, cored, and cut into thick wedges
  1 cantaloupe, peeled, seeded, and cut into bite-size cubes
  ¼ ripe watermelon (or appropriate amount of other fruit), cut into bite-size pieces

Skewer the fruit in the order listed for individual servings. Place the skewers in a basket lined with leaves and chill until serving time. Decorate the basket with flowers.

To Prepare in Advance: Cover with damp towels and chill up to 12 hours.

 *Frances's Fudge Muffins*

MAKES 36 TO 40 MUFFINS

This recipe comes from our recipe-swapping pal, Frances Pelham.

  2 cups (4 sticks) unsalted butter
  2 bars (4 ounces each) sweet chocolate
3½ cups sugar
  2 cups sifted unbleached all-purpose flour
  1 tablespoon cocoa

8 eggs
2 teaspoons vanilla
⅛ teaspoon salt
4 cups chopped walnuts

Preheat oven to 300°F and set rack in the center of the oven. Line muffin tins with paper muffin cups.

Melt butter and chocolate together in a heavy pan over very low heat; set aside. In a large mixing bowl combine the sugar, flour, and cocoa. Stir in the chocolate mixture. Add the eggs, vanilla, and salt, whisking just until well combined; do not overbeat. Fill muffin cups ⅔ full. Bake for 40 minutes or until firm when lightly pressed.

To Prepare in Advance: Cool the muffins and freeze. To reheat, thaw and wrap all the muffins in a large bundle with foil; heat for 20 minutes at 375°F.

A LIGHT ORIENTAL MENU
(FOR 4)

Japanese Green Tea

---

*Tray of Sushi Garnished with Exotic Flowers
and Enoki Mushrooms:*

Kappamaki (Cucumber Sushi Rolls)

California Rolls

Cucumber Flowers Filled with Salmon Roe

Oriental Fruits on a Mound of Ice

A   LIGHT   ORIENTAL   MENU

As children we would stay in the water until our fingers and toes turned wrinkled and white and our bodies accommodated themselves to the water's temperature. We felt far more comfortable in than out, and would have preferred to skip the sandy picnic and stay in the water all day.

The weightless pleasures of being semi-submerged still beckon to us as they did in childhood. If you can't escape to the beach or a lake, it's possible to avoid the wind and the sand entirely by sharing a backyard hot tub with your friends. As you relax there, watching the steamy vapors curling lightly upwards, you realize that one of the advantages of growing up is that you can still have white, wrinkled fingers and toes—without getting out of the water for lunch.

There is, as yet, no definitive answer as to what would be the proper food to feed a sybaritic hot-tub lounger. The question is all too new. It must be finger food, certainly, but what kind? Long-stemmed Belgian white asparagus, braised and dressed in vinaigrette, would unfortunately tend to drip. Phyllo-wrapped Greek *tyropitas* would flake and absorb moisture from wet hands. We have settled on an arrangement of sushi, including Kappamaki (cucumber roll) and California Rolls (the same as Kappamaki, but filled with cooked crabmeat and avocado), served directly on a large moisture-proof tray. They are accompanied by cucumber flowers holding a teaspoon each of salmon caviar in their shallow centers. We would serve hot unsweetened green tea accompanied by lychees, Japanese snow peaches, thinly sliced melon and other available fruits served on a decorative bed of shaved ice.

This menu may be used, of course, in another setting, but without the warmth of the hot tub, you might want to wait for summer.

SHOPPING LIST

From an Oriental market

- 1 package *nori* (8 or more sheets)
- 1 can snow peaches
- 1 can lychees
- Japanese soy sauce
- ¼ cup *wasabe* powder
- Japanese rice vinegar (unseasoned)
- Pickled ginger *(amazu shoga)*
- 1 bag fresh *enoki* mushrooms
- Green tea
- ¼ cup *sake* (or 2 tablespoons *mirin*)
- Bamboo sushi mat (optional)

From the supermarket

- 2 Japanese or hothouse cucumbers
- 1 ripe avocado
- 1 orange *or* canned mandarin orange sections
- 1 basket fresh berries
- Grapes
- 1 or 2 halved melons, as available
- 4 ounces cooked shredded crabmeat
- 2 ounces red salmon roe
- 3 cups short-grain rice
- 10 cups shaved ice

Staples

- Sugar (¼ cup)
- Salt (1½ teaspoons)
- Sesame seed (3 tablespoons)

DO-AHEAD TIMETABLE

One day ahead: Prepare ice for dessert and keep frozen

Day of the party: Cut cucumber flowers. Make sushi rice (up to 3 hours ahead)

Just before the party: Mix *wasabe*. Make sushi rolls. Fill cucumber flowers with salmon roe. Complete and garnish serving tray

During the party: Brew green tea. Place fruits on ice

 *Japanese Green Tea*

FOR 4 TO 5 SINGLE SERVINGS

Japanese tea is green, unlike the fermented black teas usually served in China and the West. It is usually served unsweetened in handleless mugs. The green tea most commonly found in Oriental markets and many supermarkets is *bancha*. Another type that we particularly enjoy is *genmai-cha*—the same tea, but with tiny kernels of popped rice which add a nutty flavor.

To make 4 to 5 cups of tea place 1 tablespoon bancha or genmai-cha leaves into a warm teapot. Add a cup of hot but not boiling water and let steep for 1 minute. Pour into warm cups. Repeat the addition of water to the same tea, let steep 1 minute, and pour again.

 *Sushi*

In recent years sushi restaurants have become increasingly popular in the large metropolitan areas of the United States. Many people approach them with some trepidation, but both experienced and fledgling sushi eaters will appreciate this menu since we have chosen sushi featuring flavors other than raw fish. Japanese ingredients such as rice vinegar, *nori* (seaweed wrapper), and *wasabe* (green horseradish powder) have become widely available and may even be purchased through mail order by those who do not live in large cities.

Kappamaki (Cucumber Sushi Rolls)

FOR 4 ROLLS OR 24 PIECES

4   sheets *nori* (see Note 1)
1   recipe Easy Sushi Rice (page 36)
     "Hand vinegar," consisting of 1 teaspoon Japanese rice
         vinegar mixed with 3 tablespoons cold water
2   tablespoons *wasabe* (see Note 2), mixed to a paste with a small
         amount of cold water
½   Japanese or hothouse cucumber, cut into 3-inch sections, then
         into fine julienne strips
4   teaspoons sesame seeds toasted in a dry skillet until golden

TO SERVE:

Japanese soy sauce
Any remaining wasabe paste

Note 1: These thin sheets of dark green or purplish dried seaweed, used to make *maki-* or rolled-type sushi, are available in plastic packages or in cans. Measuring about 7x8 inches, the sheets resemble carbon paper. Packaged nori labeled *yakinori* is pre-toasted; that labeled *ajitsuke-nori* is seasoned with soy sauce. The flavor will be enhanced if you toast the shiny side of a sheet just before use by holding it with tongs and waving it over a gas flame until it becomes greenish and crisp. Store unused nori in an airtight container in the freezer, along with the moisture-absorbing granules with which it was originally packed, and use the remainder soon, as it loses flavor on standing.

Note 2: Wasabe is an extremely hot green horseradish powder sold in small tins in Oriental markets. Mix the powder with just enough water to make a smooth paste; cover and let stand for 10 minutes to allow the flavor to develop fully. The paste is smeared on rice when making sushi, and served as a condiment with soy sauce for diners to flavor their own dipping sauce. Powdered wasabe may be stored on the pantry shelf for years, but once mixed to a paste with water it should be served within a few hours.

It is easiest to use a bamboo sushi mat to make these rolls, but a small kitchen towel may be used if necessary. Toast a sheet of *nori* by holding it with tongs and waving it over a gas flame for a few seconds until light greenish and crisp. Place it shiny side down on the mat, a short side nearest you. Dip your fingers in "hand vinegar" and spread the rice approximately ½ inch thick over the seaweed, covering ¾ of it and leaving ¼ (the end furthest from you) uncovered. Spread some wasabe paste in a strip across the center of the rice (it is very pungent, so don't overdo). Lay some cucumber strips on top of the wasabe and sprinkle lightly with toasted sesame seed. Lift the closest edge of nori up and over the filling just to meet the other edge of nori beyond the far edge of the rice, using the mat to roll it very tightly. (This may take a bit of practice, but mistakes are edible.)

Remove from the mat and use a very sharp slicing knife to cut the roll in half crosswise. Cut each half into three pieces, approximately 1 inch wide. Repeat until all rice and nori are used.

Arrange the slices cut side up on a serving tray. Serve with small individual dishes of soy sauce and wasabe paste for dipping.

To Prepare in Advance: Sushi rolls are best freshly made and eaten while the rice is still slightly warm. They may be covered with plastic wrap and left at room temperature or placed in the refrigerator for up to 8 hours, though the nori loses crispness on standing.

California Rolls

MAKES 4 ROLLS OR 24 PIECES

4   sheets *nori* (see Note 1 in preceding recipe)
1   recipe Easy Sushi Rice (page 36)
    "Hand vinegar," consisting of 1 teaspoon Japanese rice
        vinegar mixed with 3 tablespoons cold water
2   tablespoons *wasabe* (see Note 2 in preceding recipe), mixed to
        a paste with a small amount of water
½   ripe avocado, peeled, pitted, and cut into fine lengthwise
        strips
4   ounces cooked shredded crabmeat
4   teaspoons sesame seed, toasted in a dry skillet until golden

TO SERVE:

Japanese soy sauce
Any remaining wasabe paste

Make these in the same manner as the Cucumber Sushi Rolls, using strips of avocado and shredded crabmeat in place of the cucumber strips.

 ## Easy Sushi Rice

MAKES 4 CUPS, TO FILL 4 ROLLS

The traditional way to make sushi rice is to slowly add sweetened vinegar and seasonings to cooked rice, fanning it constantly to give it a lustrous appearance. This easy method produces a good result, the only difference being that the rice is less shiny. This amount is sufficient for 24 cut pieces of sushi, either Cucumber Rolls or California Rolls. The recipe may be doubled or halved.

1½	cups raw short-grain rice (such as Calrose)
1½	cups water
¼	cup Japanese rice vinegar (*su*) (see Note 1)
2	tablespoons sugar
2	tablespoons *sake or* 1 tablespoon *mirin* (see Note 2)
¾	teaspoon salt

Note 1: Most supermarkets now carry several kinds of rice vinegars, which are lighter and sweeter than Western-style vinegars. Marukan and Mitsukan are the most widely known brands. Buy the plain (green label) rather than the seasoned (orange label) type, which has added sugar, salt, and monosodium glutamate.

Note 2: Sake is Japanese rice wine, which is heated for drinking and is also used extensively in cooking. It is widely available in liquor stores. *Mirin* is a sweet, syrupy rice wine that is used only in cooking. It is sold in Oriental markets and many supermarkets. If storing *mirin* longer than a few months, keep it in the refrigerator.

Rinse rice in a strainer under cold water until the water runs clear; drain. Bring 1½ cups water to boil in heavy saucepan. Stir in rice, cover, and simmer over low heat for 15 minutes, or until the water has been absorbed. Stir in remaining ingredients, toss, and let stand, covered, for 15 minutes. The rice should be used within a few hours.

Cucumber Flowers Filled with Salmon Roe

FOR 4 TO 5 SERVINGS

This is a lovely garnish that is useful for adding height to a plate and can be filled with any number of delicious things—tangy dips, tartar sauce, or chutney, for example. Filled with salmon roe, the flowers make a great addition to a tray of sushi.

1 hothouse cucumber (see Note)
2 ounces red salmon roe

Note: We prefer to use hothouse cucumbers, found in plastic wrappers in the produce section of most markets. They seem to be less waxy and more flavorful than standard cucumbers; however, they too have their minor drawbacks. They are often far too curved for use in making this garnish, and the small end is sometimes triangular rather than round. We bring this up only to caution you in your selection. Each cucumber should provide at least 5 flowers, their size determined by the vegetable's diameter.

Wrap a thin wire (such as the type found in a box of plastic bags) around the cucumber 1½ inches from the end and secure it snugly.

Using a thin, sharp knife, cut a 1½-inch petal downward, allowing the knife blade to stop when it comes to the wire. Cut another petal to the right, overlapping the first petal by about ¼-inch. Continue cutting petals until you've gone completely around the cucumber. Petals should be paper thin at the top tapering to about ½-inch thick at the bottom. Hold both ends of the cucumber firmly with both hands and twist the flowers from the end of the cucumber.

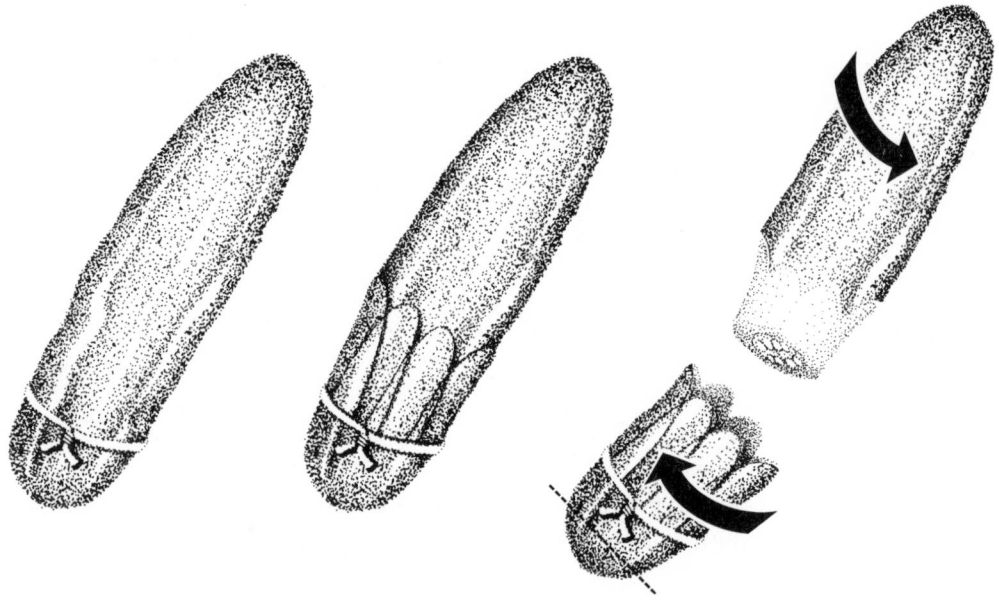

Remove the wire and trim the bottom of the flower flat, being careful not to trim too closely to where the wire was or the petals will break off. Replace wire on cucumber above last row of petals, and repeat procedure for next flower. Turn upside down and gently press the flower upside down on the tabletop to open the petals further.

Just before serving, fill the center of the cucumber flowers with 2 to 3 teaspoons of salmon roe.

To Prepare in Advance: Place the cucumber flowers upside down on a wet paper towel in a shallow pan. Cover with plastic wrap and refrigerate for up to 24 hours.

Oriental Fruits on a Mound of Ice

FOR 4 SERVINGS

Specific amounts of fruit are not given, so improvise with those that are available and most appealing.

> 10 cups shaved ice
> Canned snow peaches, drained (see Note)
> Canned lychees, drained
> Fresh orange sections *or* canned mandarin oranges, drained
> Fresh berries and grapes, as available
> Assorted melons, as available

Note: Snow peaches are canned white peach halves available in Oriental markets. Cling peach halves may be substituted.

Mound the shaved ice in a clear salad bowl to look somewhat like a conical, snow-covered mountain. Arrange the fruits on the ice, using skewers if necessary to hold them in place. Eat with chopsticks, fingers, or small forks.

To Prepare in Advance: Mound the ice in the bowl and store in the freezer up to 24 hours before serving. Cover with fruit within 2 hours of serving and store in the refrigerator. Tip out any accumulated water from melting ice before serving.

AN OUTDOOR WEDDING FEAST
(FOR 24)

Chilled Champagne or Sparkling Wine

Golden Caviar Spread

Stuffed Chicken Breasts Rockefeller

Artichoke Mushroom Salad

Red Pepper Shells with Cheese

"Stained Glass Window" Wedding Cake

AN OUTDOOR WEDDING FEAST

We have a great affection for the sophisticated and picturesque city of San Francisco, built on steep hills between the mountains and the sea. On top of one of these hills is a favorite hotel, the Stanford Court. A little over a year ago, we noticed from our window on the third floor an attractive doll-like three-story townhouse—80 feet deep, but only 20 feet wide, with a "for sale" sign in the corner of its lowest street window. We fell in love with that townhouse, and, as those in love often do, we played "What if?"—a romantic but hopeless game.

The next time we were in San Francisco we were crushed to learn that "our" townhouse had been sold.

One of the surprising delights of a subsequent trip was to find that the house had been smartly restored. Its freshly painted, fenced, and white-graveled flat roof was being prepared for a wedding. A portion of the rooftop had been covered with rolls of artificial grass. In the center of this small grassed area was a white canvas canopy, under which were placed two pink Thai silk cushions. From the tops of the supporting poles of the canopy, playing in the light winds, were green and white balloons and billowing ribbons. There were stacks of chairs on the rooftop, and the long reception tables were already in place and waiting to be covered. It was obviously to be a small buffet reception. What a marvelously ingenious place for an outdoor wedding and reception, right in the center of town. We were compelled to admire the new owners.

Our schedule did not permit us to stay and snoop, so we don't know how many were invited nor what was served. But we naturally continued our game of "What if?" and devised a menu for the fantasy affair. A buffet for 24 would be accompanied by a continuous pouring of Chandon Blanc de Noirs from the Napa Valley. Handsomely garnished Golden Caviar Spread would whet the guests' appetites for a buffet of Stuffed Chicken Breasts Rockefeller, Artichoke Mushroom Salad, and stuffed Red Pepper Shells with Cheese. The climax would be wedding cake formed of layers of Grand Marnier custard and fresh fruit.

It would have pleased us to have been invited to such a celebration as this.

SHOPPING LIST

- 10 red bell peppers
- 3 to 4 heads Belgian endive (optional)
- 1 bunch celery
- 3 bunches scallions
- 1 to 2 heads Boston, butter, or Bibb lettuce (20 to 24 leaves)
- 1 pound small white mushrooms
- 2 to 3 bunches basil (1 cup leaves)—if making fresh pesto
- 3 bunches parsley
- 1 bunch watercress
- 1 bunch chives
  Fresh thyme (1 tablespoon leaves)
- 6 baskets fresh strawberries
- 1 orange (preferably navel)
- 1 peach (freestone, not cling)
- 1 banana
- 1 kiwi
- 10 to 12 seedless green grapes
- 8 to 10 fresh blackberries, boysenberries, or purple grapes
- 2 lemons (for juice)
- 12 whole chicken breasts (24 halves), boned and split
- 2 pounds cream cheese
- 1½ pounds ricotta cheese
- 1¼ pounds mozzarella cheese, shredded
  Parmesan cheese (for ¼ cup grated *plus* ⅓ cup if making fresh pesto)
- 2 sticks butter

- 2 cups (16 ounces) heavy cream
- 2 cups (16 ounces) sour cream
- 2 cups (16 ounces) milk
- 13 eggs
- 8 ounces golden caviar
- 4 packages (10 ounces each) frozen chopped spinach
- ½ cup frozen pesto (if not making fresh)
- 2 pounds frozen pound cake
- 4 cans (14 ounces each) artichoke bottoms (not hearts)
  Cracottes (or other plain crackers) for serving caviar spread
- 1 loaf white sandwich bread (preferably Pepperidge Farm)
- 2 tablespoons pine nuts or walnuts (if making fresh pesto)
- 4 envelopes unflavored gelatin
- ½ cup apple juice
  About ⅓ cup Grand Marnier
- 3 tablespoons Pernod (or substitute 2 teaspoons anise seed)
- 16 to 20 bottles Champagne or sparkling white wine
  Ice to chill Champagne

Staples

Olive oil (¼ cup plus ¼ cup if making fresh pesto)
Garlic (3 cloves)
Sugar (1¼ cups)
Tabasco sauce
Vanilla (1 tablespoon)

Dried thyme (1 teaspoon, if
    fresh not available)
Anise seed (2 teaspoons, if
    Pernod not available)
Dry mustard (2 teaspoons)
Paprika
Salt
White pepper

From a hobby shop

1 yard clear acetate, 2½ to 2¾
    inches wide
Double-face transparent tape

From the garden, nursery, or florist

Nasturtiums or rose, to garnish
    caviar spread

DO-AHEAD TIMETABLE

Three days ahead: Prepare base of caviar mold. Prepare stuffing

Two days ahead: Assemble wedding cake without final glaze

One day ahead: Glaze wedding cake. Assemble salads without dressing

Day of the party: Cook pepper shells

Just before the party: Ice Champagne. Frost mold with caviar and garnish
    with flowers. Top salads with dressing

During the party: Reheat chicken. Reheat pepper shells

Golden Caviar Spread

FOR 24 SERVINGS

Golden caviar (whitefish roe from North America), found in gourmet specialty shops, is mild, golden-apricot in color, and costs less than one-fourth the price of Iranian Beluga or Sevruga caviars. It also freezes beautifully. For this silky spread we use it lavishly as a sort of "frosting." Other ways we enjoy golden caviar are as a garnish on pasta with a light cream sauce and on grilled fish.

    2   pounds cream cheese
    3   tablespoons snipped fresh chives
    2   tablespoons fresh lemon juice

Salt and freshly ground white pepper
8 ounces golden caviar

TO GARNISH AND SERVE:

Fresh nontoxic flowers, such as a single rose or nasturtiums
Cracottes or other plain crackers, or leaves of Belgian endive

Combine the cream cheese with the chives, lemon juice, and salt and white pepper to taste until well blended; if using a food processor, do not overblend or the mixture will be too soft to hold its shape. Line a 9-inch quiche dish or pie plate with plastic wrap to make a mold. Pack the mixture into the mold, smooth the top, press plastic wrap into the exposed surface, and chill thoroughly.

To serve, turn out onto a serving dish and peel off the plastic wrap. Spread the caviar evenly over the cheese to cover completely. (If the caviar seems liquid, drain it briefly on paper towels.) Serve chilled.

To Prepare in Advance: The cream cheese mixture may be made several days ahead of time. Spread with caviar within 30 minutes of serving.

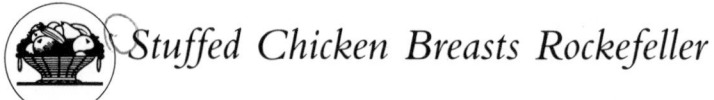

Stuffed Chicken Breasts Rockefeller

FOR 24 SERVINGS

We once prepared a chicken stuffed with zucchini and ricotta cheese from a recipe by Richard Olney. We changed the zucchini to spinach, added some New Orleans ingredients, used it to stuff boneless chicken breasts, and came up with a dish that is delicious hot or cold, all year round.

ROCKEFELLER STUFFING:

3 garlic cloves
24 scallions (including part of the green tops) *or* 4 large shallots
8 celery stalks
2 bunches parsley (leaves only)
¼ cup (½ stick) butter
4 packages (10 ounces each) frozen chopped spinach, thawed
1½ pounds ricotta cheese

6   cups fresh breadcrumbs (see Note 1)
1   tablespoon fresh thyme, chopped, *or* 1 teaspoon dried thyme, crumbled
3   tablespoons Pernod, or more to taste (or substitute—see Note 2)
    Tabasco to taste
4   eggs, beaten

12   whole chicken breasts, boned and split, (skin attached)
¼   cup (½ stick) butter, melted
¼   cup freshly grated Parmesan cheese
    Paprika
    Salt, if desired

Note 1: It is easy to make fresh breadcrumbs in a blender or food processor. We prefer Pepperidge Farm white sandwich bread or French bread for this purpose. Remove crusts and tear bread into pieces. Process (one slice at a time if using a blender) until you have fine crumbs. The crumbs freeze well.

Note 2: Pernod is an anise-flavored aperitif available in all well-stocked liquor stores. An acceptable substitute for this recipe can be made by soaking 2 teaspoons anise seed in 1½ tablespoons boiling water for 10 minutes, then straining out the seeds. Use the resulting anise-flavored tea in place of Pernod.

If you have a food processor, use it to make the stuffing. In the work bowl fitted with the steel blade, mince the garlic. Depending on the size of your processor, you may have to chop the vegetables in batches. Cut the scallions and celery stalks into 1-inch lengths (if using shallots, cut in half) and add them to the processor, chopping with on-off bursts until minced. Add the parsley leaves and process in on-off bursts until finely chopped. If not using a food processor, use a sharp knife to mince the garlic, scallions, celery, and parsley.

Preheat oven to 350°F.

Melt the butter in a heavy skillet over medium heat and sauté the chopped vegetables for 5 to 10 minutes, stirring often, until slightly softened. Meanwhile, squeeze as much liquid as possible from the thawed spinach, so it is very dry. When the onion is transparent but not browned, stir in the spinach, ricotta, breadcrumbs, thyme, Pernod or anise tea, and Tabasco. Let cool to room temperature, then stir in the beaten eggs.

To stuff the chicken breasts, use your fingers to lift the skin of the chicken on one side to form a pocket, leaving three sides as well attached as possible. Divide the stuffing evenly into 12 portions, pressing lightly between your hands to make breast-size patties. Top each piece of breast meat with stuffing, then cover with the skin.

Place stuffed chicken skin side up on foil-covered baking pans. Tuck any ragged pieces of skin underneath to make them neat looking.

Brush the skin of the chicken with melted butter. Sprinkle evenly with Parmesan, paprika, and salt, if desired. Bake for 30 minutes, or until the chicken is just done; do not overcook.

The breasts may be served hot, at room temperature, or cold.

To Prepare in Advance: The filling may be refrigerated for up to 3 days or frozen indefinitely. Stuff the chicken breasts within an hour of baking them, taking care that both stuffing and chicken are cold. The breasts may be baked the day before serving, undercooking them by about 5 minutes. Cool and refrigerate overnight. To serve hot, reheat at 300°F for about 20 minutes.

 ## Artichoke Mushroom Salad

FOR 20 TO 24 SERVINGS

We thank Jennifer Edwards, who formerly assisted us in our cooking demonstrations, for this very pretty salad. Fresh artichokes are in season in the spring.

20 to 24	medium artichokes *or* 4 cans (14 ounces each) artichoke bottoms (not hearts—see Note) *or* 20 to 24 frozen artichoke bottoms, prepared according to package directions
1	lemon, sliced (if using fresh artichokes)

SOUR CREAM DRESSING:

2	cups sour cream
2	tablespoons fresh lemon juice
2	teaspoons dry mustard
	Salt to taste

46

<pre>
        1   pound small white mushrooms
20 to 24   leaves of tender lettuce, such as Boston, butter, or Bibb
        1   bunch watercress (leaves only)
            Paprika
</pre>

Note: Artichoke bottoms are shaped like small saucers, and are the hearts without any leaves. You will find them canned, packed in water, in most supermarkets. Each 14-ounce can contains 5 to 7 artichoke bottoms.

If using fresh artichokes, trim the stems flush with the base. Use a sharp chef's knife to cut off the top ¾ of the leaves. Use a paring knife to trim away the leaves from around the base, leaving a smooth, rounded bottom. Drop into a large pot of simmering salted water to which you have added a sliced lemon. Cook just until the base of the artichokes is easily pierced with a knife. Drain and cool. Scrape out the hairy chokes with a spoon (a grapefruit spoon works well), and trim the artichoke bottoms of any remaining leaves so that they are saucer-like. If using canned or frozen artichoke hearts, simply drain and dry them well.

For dressing, combine sour cream, lemon juice, dry mustard, and salt to taste and let stand at least 20 minutes to allow the mustard flavor to develop.

Clean mushrooms with a mushroom brush or by wiping them clean with damp paper towels. Using a sharp paring knife, cut into very thin lengthwise slices.

If using canned artichoke bottoms, trim them so they stand as securely as possible. Arrange lettuce leaves on a large serving platter, one leaf for each artichoke bottom. Toss together the mushrooms and watercress leaves and use to fill the hollowed centers of the artichoke bottoms.

Spoon the dressing over the mushrooms and sprinkle the tops lightly with paprika.

To Prepare in Advance: The salad, without dressing, may be arranged on the platter up to 24 hours ahead. Cover completely with damp paper towels and refrigerate. Just before serving, top with dressing and dust with paprika. The dressing will keep for up to a week in the refrigerator, depending on the expiration date on the carton of sour cream.

 *Red Pepper Shells with Cheese*

FOR 20 SERVINGS

Halved red peppers make natural containers for melted cheese to serve as a side dish with many menus.

10 red bell peppers
5 cups (1¼ pounds) shredded mozzarella cheese
About ½ cup pesto, *or* oil from a jar of sun-dried tomatoes (see Note)

Note: Pesto is an uncooked garlic and herb sauce used in Italian cooking. It is available frozen or vacuum-packed in jars in Italian delis and some supermarkets all year. If fresh basil is available, make it quickly in the blender or food processor by combining 1 cup firmly packed fresh basil leaves, ⅓ cup freshly grated Parmesan cheese, ¼ cup parsley leaves, ¼ cup fine-quality olive oil, 2 tablespoons pine nuts or walnuts, 1 garlic clove, and ½ teaspoon salt and processing to a paste consistency. Pesto may be refrigerated for up to a week or frozen for up to 3 months. For sun-dried tomatoes, see Note 2 of the Tabouli recipe.

Preheat oven to 375°F. On a chopping board, position the peppers on their sides to see where they must be cut to hold a stable position on a plate, then cut in half lengthwise through the stems. Remove seeds and membranes, leaving the stems in place. Lay the pepper shells on their sides in an oiled shallow baking pan (rock salt or crumbled foil may be placed underneath them to hold them steady). Place about 2 tablespoons cheese in each half and drizzle with about 1 teaspoon pesto or tomato oil. Bake for 10 minutes, or until cheese is melted.
Variation: Use green bell peppers with mozzarella and substitute 1 sun-dried tomato half in place of the pesto.
To Prepare in Advance: The peppers may be cooked in the morning. Reheat in a low oven or in a microwave oven until the cheese is soft.

"Stained Glass Window" Wedding Cake

FOR UP TO 20 SERVINGS

We once saw a wedding cake topped with an arrangement of fresh fruit to resemble a stained glass window and were inspired to recreate it at home. More than the usual amount of plain gelatin is used throughout this creation so it will hold up at room temperature.

SPECIAL EQUIPMENT:

a 10-inch springform pan
1 yard clear acetate, 2½ to 2¾ inches wide (see Note)
double-face transparent tape

GRAND MARNIER CUSTARD:

3 envelopes unflavored gelatin
½ cup cold water
¼ cup Grand Marnier
9 egg yolks
1¼ cups sugar
¼ teaspoon salt
2 cups milk
1 tablespoon vanilla
2 cups heavy cream

TO ASSEMBLE AND GARNISH:

2 pounds pound cake (homemade or purchased) *or* other densely textured cake of your choice
1 to 2 tablespoons Grand Marnier
6 baskets large strawberries, hulled
1 freestone peach, blanched for 30 seconds, peeled, sliced, and brushed with lemon juice to prevent darkening

49

8 to 10   blackberries, boysenberries, or purple grapes

1   kiwi, peeled and sliced crosswise

1   ripe banana, sliced diagonally and brushed with lemon juice to prevent darkening

1   orange (preferably navel), skin and membranes removed, sectioned

10 to 12   seedless green grapes

GLAZE:

1   envelope unflavored gelatin

½   cup cold water

½   cup apple juice

Note: Clear acetate, which is much sturdier than cellophane or plastic wrap, is sold in hobby shops.

Line the side of the springform pan with the strip of acetate, securing it to itself with the double-sided adhesive tape. Make sure the bottom of the pan fits snugly onto the sides. Oil the acetate lightly so it will be easily removed from the cake. Place the pan on a square sheet of aluminum foil and bring the sides up to catch any custard that may leak out before the gelatin sets.

To make the custard, sprinkle 3 tablespoons gelatin over the water and Grand Marnier in a measuring cup; set aside. In the top of a double boiler (or in a 3-quart glass measure if you have a microwave oven) beat the egg yolks for 1 minute, then gradually beat in the sugar. Bring the milk just to a boil in a saucepan, then beat it gradually into the yolks. Place the mixture over boiling water and cook it for 5 minutes, stirring often (or cook at high power in a microwave oven for 1½ minutes, stirring every 30 seconds). The custard will not thicken during this time, but the sugar will dissolve and the yolks will lose any raw flavor.

Remove from the heat and stir in the softened gelatin and vanilla. Chill, stirring from time to time, until custard thickens but is not yet firmly set. Whip the cream just until it holds soft peaks and fold it into the custard mixture. Set aside.

To assemble the cake, cut ¾ of the pound cake into ½-inch slices and use the slices, trimmed as necessary, to completely cover the bottom of the prepared pan. Sprinkle the cake layer very lightly with about a tablespoon of Grand Marnier. Halve some of the strawberries lengthwise and arrange them on top of

the cake around the side of the prepared pan, cut side out and large ends down, pressing them firmly against the acetate. Carefully pour in some of the custard to just cover the cake layer and the lower third of the strawberries. Quarter 3 or 4 strawberries lengthwise and arrange them in a single layer over the custard, letting them sink in. Chill until firm, at least 30 minutes. Let the remaining custard stand at room temperature, so it doesn't set until you pour the final layer on the cake.

Make a second layer of pound cake (this time it need not fit exactly, and you can stud any small spaces with cut strawberries) and pour 1 cup of custard over that. Chill again just until firm.

Sprinkle any exposed cake lightly with another tablespoon of Grand Marnier. Make a final layer of cake, slicing it only ¼-inch thick and piecing it evenly as you did the first layer. Spread any remaining custard over the top and chill at least 2 hours, until very firm.

To decorate the top of the cake you will need to make a firm gelatin glaze—twice as firm as usual, so it will hold up at room temperature. Sprinkle the gelatin over ¼ cup cold water in a heatproof 1-cup glass measure and let stand for 3 minutes or longer. Heat briefly in microwave or in hot bath on range top until the mixture is clear and liquid. Add ½ cup apple juice and another ¼ cup cold water and stir to blend. Chill for 15 minutes or so, until slightly syrupy. (If you let it stand too long glaze will become too thick to brush, and will have to be remelted and cooled again before you proceed.)

Remove the sides of the springform pan so you can see through the acetate where the strawberries are positioned on the side of the cake. Halve most of the remaining strawberries lengthwise (reserving a perfect one for the center of the cake) and position them cut side down around the top of the cake, with pointed ends protruding ½-inch or so beyond the edge; they should match up as much as possible with the cut strawberries on the sides (see photograph). Spoon one layer of gelatin glaze over the strawberries. (The springform side may now be repositioned around the cake to protect it.) For the next row, working toward the center of the cake, alternate peach slices and blackberries or purple grapes. Brush this row with gelatin and give the rim of strawberries a second coat. For the third row, alternate kiwi slices, banana, and orange sections. Brush with glaze. Place a whole perfect strawberry, stem end down, in the center of the cake, surrounding it with "petals" of halved strawberries pointing outwards and meeting the row of banana and kiwi. Fill the space between the center strawberry and petals with peach slices. Surround the center strawberry with fresh raspberries

or with seedless green grapes (feel free to improvise here with available fruit to make the cake your own creation). Brush several layers of gelatin over the fruit on top the cake, to glaze and secure it and also to prevent the bananas and peaches from darkening.

Just before serving, use a sharp knife or scissors to cut through the strip of acetate; discard it. Cut cake in slices to serve.

To Prepare in Advance: Assemble the cake, without fruit topping and glaze, no more than 48 hours before serving. Top with fruit and glaze within 24 hours of serving. Keep chilled as long as possible, though the cake will hold up well at room temperature (in a cool place) for at least 3 hours.

SUMMER

SUMMER is the most exuberant season, offering warm luxuriant days and balmy nights, baseball in the park, and an abundance of fresh produce in the markets.

Dining alfresco becomes a way of life for us, and we eat outdoors at every opportunity. In the garden fresh fruits and flowers are growing in abundance. We cook simple and sensual menus, decorating platters of cold food with nasturtiums, pansies, and all kinds of herb flowers. Our tomato crop provides us with a continual bounty of vine-ripened sweetness.

In the produce sections of markets we fall in love all over again with lush fruits—peaches, cherries, nectarines, grapes, plums, apricots, pineapples. Strawberries are a great bargain and we binge on them almost daily, eating them plain, as a filling for buttery shortcake, and in uncooked strawberry jam. The first of the season go into our Rumtopf, a crockery canister with a loose-fitting lid that we stir daily and keep in a cool place. Four cups of small, fresh strawberries are mixed with 4 cups sugar and macerated for an hour to two, then covered with a quart of brandy and allowed to soak for about a week. From time to time throughout the summer we add 4 cups of any of the previously listed fruits, pitted if necessary and cut up along with an equal weight of sugar, stirring once a day for at least a week after the addition of more fruit to dissolve the sugar. It it not necessary to add more brandy as the fruit produces its own wine as it ages. At the beginning of October, when the fruit has aged at least a month after the addition of the last fruit, we ladle the mixture into jars and store it in a cool place or the refrigerator, to appear later as a dessert on its own or as a sauce for ice cream.

The wild, frosty pink color of watermelon is almost as enchanting as the taste. And soft fruits, too colorful for our Rumtopf mixture, are beautiful additions to many summer menus.

This being the season for shellfish, we plan a beach cookout of paella, the Spanish national dish, a mixture of rice and spicy sausages, meats, and shellfish. Seldom does summer pass without at least one evening under the stars at an outdoor concert, and we are delighted with the menu we've planned for that occasion around fresh berries, herbs, and the first June peas. Parks are popular now, and we see families there at play, enjoying each other and each other's food offerings, so we are inspired to plan a family reunion for the Fourth of July with a few friends tossed in for fun. On Bastille Day, usually one of the warmer days of the year, we create a French picnic and drink a toast to Canon Kir, who inspired the drink named after him, and the French for inventing *le pique-nique*.

Another summer activity is a day of sailing, so we plan a menu we can make the day before and pack in a hurry in case someone asks us to crew. Our fantasy picnic this month is one we would love to eat while viewing land from a hot-air balloon, but which will taste just as good in a meadow or wooded glen.

It is a season of outrageous freshness, luxuriant meadows, a celebration of colors, fragrances, and outdoor living.

AN EVENING COOKOUT
AT THE BEACH, SPANISH STYLE
(FOR 8 TO 10)

Chilled fruity white wine or beer

Gazpacho

Paella with Chicken, Seafood, and Grilled Sausages

Crusty French Bread

Broccoli with Olive Oil and Garlic

Spanish Cream with Sangría Fruit

54

AN EVENING COOKOUT
AT THE BEACH, SPANISH STYLE

We have never unraveled the mystery of why it is so stimulating to the appetite to eat under the stars by the seaside. But it is a simple fact that appetites and spirits become more playful as daylight wanes.

This menu is one that is easily transportable. After the perfect site is chosen, the bar is set up. With cup in hand and perhaps a few extemporaneous toasts and speeches to sunsets, the joy of life, and companionship, a fire is prepared. Now is the time to serve Gazpacho, that delicious, chunky Spanish soup that may be sipped or eaten with a spoon.

If the sun has not yet set, there will be time for people to go off on their own, some, hand-in-hand, to the water's edge, some to explore the dunes. Others, if a football is handy, exhaust themselves with yelling and falling down. At the beach, unfortunately, more than in other eating-out situations, cookout preparation becomes a one- or two-person operation: you are forewarned. If your department of parks and recreation will permit an open wood fire, you're lucky. If not, a charcoal brazier or a Japanese *hibachi* will work just as well. We like to bring most of our food already prepared to keep things as simple as possible. Paella, a Spanish dish of rice and assorted seafood, poultry, sausage, and vegetables, is a zesty one-pot main course that is perfect for hearty appetites. It is accompanied by crusty bread.

The dessert, already in its serving glasses, is a delicate, vanilla-flavored cream topped with a sauce inspired by the traditional Spanish wine-and-fruit drink, sangría.

If you are lucky enough to have a full moon, you're very fortunate indeed. If you also have among your guests a friend who plays a romantic Spanish guitar, you are even more so.

¡Con mucho gusto!

SHOPPING LIST

2 pounds tomatoes
1 large tomato or 12 cherry
  tomatoes
5 to 6 pounds fresh broccoli
6 baby artichokes (if using fresh)
1 large onion
2 celery stalks
1 medium cucumber
2 medium-size red bell peppers
2 medium-size green bell peppers
1 bunch scallions
  Fresh oregano (1 tablespoon
    chopped)
  Fresh coriander (cilantro; 1 to 2
    teaspoons chopped),
    optional
  Fresh thyme (1½ teaspoons)
  Fresh parsley
2 lemons
1 large orange
1 lime
¼ ripe pineapple
1 cup seedless grapes
1 peach or nectarine (freestone,
  not cling)
8 to 10 chicken legs or thighs
1 pound spicy sausages (Spanish,
  not Mexican, *chorizo* or
  Polish *kielbasa*)
1 cup (8 ounces) heavy cream
1 cup (8 ounces) sour cream
½ package (5 ounces) frozen peas

1 package (10 ounces) frozen artichoke hearts (if not using
  fresh)
2 cups converted rice
2 baguettes or other loaves of
  crusty bread
1 envelope unflavored gelatin
½ cup slivered almonds
5 cups beef broth
2 cups chicken broth
1 can (28 ounces) crushed
  tomatoes in tomatoes puree
  (if not using fresh tomatoes)
1 can (46 ounces) tomato juice
9 ounces red wine vinegar
10 to 12 pimiento-stuffed green
  olives
10 to 12 pitted black olives
½ teaspoon saffron threads
1½ cups olive oil
1 cup dry white wine
½ cup red wine or tawny Port

From the fish market

24 fresh clams and/or mussels
1 pound cooked large shrimp

Staples

Worcestershire sauce (2
  tablespoons)
Tabasco sauce
Vanilla (1½ teaspoons)
Sugar (½ cup)
Superfine sugar (1 tablespoon)

Garlic (6 cloves)
Bay leaves (2)
Coriander (¼ teaspoon ground
    or crushed seeds)
Dried oregano (1 teaspoon, if
    fresh not available)
Dried thyme (½ teaspoon, if
    fresh not available)

Turmeric (½ teaspoon)
Paprika
Cayenne pepper (⅛ teaspoon)
Salt
Black pepper

DO-AHEAD TIMETABLE

Up to a month ahead: Make and freeze sauce base for paella

Three days ahead: Make gazpacho

Two days ahead: Cook broccoli. Prepare Spanish cream; chill

Day of the party: Chill white wine or beer. Marinate sangría fruit

Just before leaving for the picnic: Pack ice chests

At the beach: Finish cooking paella, adding all toppings. Heat bread

---

 *Gazpacho*

FOR 8 TO 10 SERVINGS

There are many versions of this refreshing chunky soup/salad, and this has become our family's favorite.

2 pounds ripe tomatoes (plum or vine-ripened preferred),
    peeled, seeded, and diced *or* 1 can (28 ounces)
    crushed tomatoes in tomato puree
1 can (46 ounces) tomato juice
1 cup red wine vinegar
3 tablespoons olive oil (extra-virgin preferred)
1 tablespoon chopped fresh oregano *or* 1 teaspoon dried
    oregano leaves, crumbled

   1   medium-size red and 1 medium-size green bell pepper
          (or 2 green bell peppers), seeds and mem-
          branes removed, finely diced
   1   medium cucumber, peeled, seeded, and finely diced
   2   celery stalks, finely diced
   6   scallions (including part of the green tops), thinly sliced
   2   garlic cloves, minced or pressed
        Salt and Tabasco to taste
1 to 2   teaspoons chopped fresh coriander (cilantro), optional

Combine all ingredients, seasoning to taste with salt and Tabasco. Chill in a large nonmetal container for several hours.

To serve, ladle into glasses or mugs.

To Prepare in Advance: Store in the refrigerator for up to 3 days.

 ## *Paella with Chicken, Seafood, and Grilled Sausages*

FOR 8 TO 10 SERVINGS

Paella is a traditional Spanish rice dish which derives its name from the round pan with handles in which it is cooked and served. It has an infinite number of variations, using whatever seafood, poultry, meats, and vegetables are available. This recipe is adapted from our first cookbook, *The Pleasure of Your Company* (Atheneum).

    2   tablespoons olive oil
    1   large onion, sliced
    2   medium-size green or red bell peppers, seeds and mem-
          branes removed, sliced into rings
8 to 10 chicken legs or thighs
   ½   cup olive oil
    2   cups raw converted rice

SAUCE BASE:

5 cups beef broth

2 cups chicken broth

1 cup dry white wine

1 tablespoon red wine vinegar

2 garlic cloves, minced or pressed

½ teaspoon paprika

½ teaspoon saffron threads (see Note 1)

½ teaspoon turmeric

2 teaspoons chopped fresh oregano *or* ½ teaspoon dried oregano, crumbled

1½ teaspoons fresh thyme *or* ½ teaspoon dried thyme, crumbled

¼ teaspoon ground coriander *or* crushed coriander seed

2 bay leaves

⅛ teaspoon cayenne pepper

Salt and freshly ground black pepper to taste

GARNISHES:

6 baby artichokes *or* 1 package (10 ounces) frozen artichoke hearts, partially thawed

½ package (5 ounces) frozen peas, thawed

1 large tomato, peeled, seeded, and chopped *or* 12 cherry tomatoes, halved

1 pound cooked large shrimp

20 clams and/or mussels, soaked in cold water and scrubbed clean

1 pound highly-seasoned *cooked* pork sausages of your choice (see Note 2)

¼ cup toasted slivered almonds

10 to 12 pimiento-stuffed olives

10 to 12 pitted black olives

2 tablespoons chopped fresh parsley

Note 1: You can find saffron in gourmet specialty shops, fish markets, and many ethnic markets. If you don't see it be sure to ask for it, because it is usually kept in a dark place. Beware of the spice sold in Latin American markets under the

name "Mexican saffron" or *azafrán,* which is not saffron but safflower.
Note 2: Spanish-style *chorizo* is the authentic choice. Avoid Mexican-style chorizo, which is crumbly and oily, and difficult to cook and slice. *Kielbasa,* a Polish sausage flavored with garlic, is good here too.

You will need a large paella pan or attractive skillet for the final assembly and serving of this entree.

Heat 2 tablespoons olive oil in a heavy large skillet. Sauté the sliced onion and bell peppers, stirring to prevent scorching, for 10 minutes. Set aside.

Meanwhile, dry the chicken pieces very well. Heat ½ cup olive oil in a second large skillet and brown the thighs lightly on all sides. Pour out all the fat, then add the sautéed onion and bell peppers to the skillet with the chicken. Stir in all the sauce base ingredients and bring to a boil over high heat. Lower the heat, cover the skillet, and simmer slowly for 15 minutes. Remove bay leaves. (This mixture, the complete base for your paella, may be cooled to room temperature, then covered and refrigerated or frozen until needed.)

If using fresh baby artichokes, trim the stems flush with the base, remove tough outer leaves, and cook them in a large nonaluminum pot of boiling salted water to which you have added a sliced lemon, just until bottoms are tender when pierced with a fork. Drain, cool, and halve lengthwise.

When you are ready for the final cooking, be sure to have all the garnishes within arm's reach. About 20 minutes before serving, pour the chicken and its sauce into a 6-quart or larger paella pan or skillet set over a very hot fire or coals and bring to a rapid boil. Sprinkle in the rice and mix it down into the liquid with the back of a spoon. Let boil rapidly for 5 to 6 minutes; do not cover the pan or stir, or the rice will become gummy.

Arrange the peas, artichoke hearts, and tomato over the rice and press them down into the rice with a spoon, still taking care not to stir. Cook for 10 minutes, or until the rice is tender and most of the liquid is absorbed. (If the heat under the pan becomes too hot, move the pan to the side of the fire and rotate it every minute or so to prevent scorching. If the fire is too low, fan the flames or add some wood to create more intense heat. This can be a bit challenging, but is part of the excitement.) Top with the cooked shrimp and reduce the heat to very low.

Meanwhile, in a separate saucepan with a lid, simmer the mussels or clams in ½ inch of water just until they open, 5 to 10 minutes. Remove those that have opened after 10 minutes and continue cooking any that are still closed. (Discard any that do not open after 15 minutes.) Grill the sausages over direct heat until they are heated through. Place the mussels or clams on top of the paella, open

side up. Cut the grilled sausages diagonally into bite-size pieces and add them. Finish the paella by topping with the remaining garnishes. Serve immediately with crusty French bread.

To Prepare in Advance: The chicken and its seasoned cooking liquid may be prepared ahead of time at your convenience and refrigerated for up to 3 days or frozen. If necessary, the finished paella may be kept warm over very low heat for up to 30 minutes.

 ## Broccoli with Olive Oil and Garlic

FOR 8 TO 10 SERVINGS

Italian cookbook author Giuliano Bugialli describes a Florentine "stir-sauté" method for spinach. We like to use this finishing touch for many green vegetables, especially broccoli, a delicious accompaniment to this menu.

> 3   bunches (about 5 to 6 pounds) broccoli
> ⅓   cup olive oil (extra-virgin preferred)
> 2   garlic cloves, minced
>   Salt and freshly ground black pepper to taste

Wash the broccoli and cut it about 3 inches below the top of the florets. (Save the stems to use, peeled, in soups or stir-fry dishes.) Peel the stems of the florets by inserting a sharp paring knife at the base and pulling up—this removes the tough outer skin and makes the stems particularly tender. If any of the florets are very large, cut in half or quarters, as appropriate. Blanch the broccoli in boiling salted water for 3 to 4 minutes or steam in a rack over boiling water for about 8 minutes, as you prefer. Drain and blot dry.

In a large skillet, heat the olive oil with the garlic and cook over medium heat until the garlic has turned a light tan; no darker, or it will become bitter. Add the broccoli and stir-fry for 5 minutes or so, just until tender. Remove from heat and season to taste. Transfer to a serving dish or refrigerator container for storage. Serve at room temperature.

To Prepare in Advance: When cool, cover and store in the refrigerator for up to 3 days. Bring to room temperature before serving.

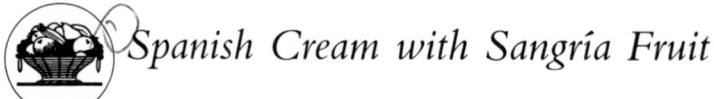

Spanish Cream with Sangría Fruit

FOR 8 TO 10 SERVINGS

Sangría, the traditional Spanish drink of red wine and seasonal fruits, here becomes a fresh-tasting dessert sauce for a vanilla mousse.

2	teaspoons unflavored gelatin
¾	cup cold water
1	cup heavy cream
½	cup sugar
1½	teaspoons vanilla
1	cup sour cream

SANGRÍA FRUIT:

	Grated rind of 1 large orange
1	large orange, peeled and sectioned
¼	ripe pineapple, cut into thin wedges
1	cup seedless grapes, halved
1	freestone peach *or* nectarine, peeled, pitted, and cut into wedges
	Juice of 1 large lime *or* ½ lemon
1	tablespoon superfine sugar
¼	cup red wine *or* tawny Port

To make the Spanish cream, stir the gelatin into ¾ cup cold water in a small saucepan. Heat just until the gelatin dissolves, then set aside to cool.

In a large mixing bowl beat the cream, sugar, and vanilla just until it holds soft peaks; do not beat until stiff. Thoroughly stir the cooled gelatin into the sour cream. Fold the sour cream mixture into the whipped cream until well combined. Spoon the Spanish cream into serving glasses, leaving room for the fruit topping.

To make the Sangría fruit, combine all the ingredients. Cover and chill for 2 to 3 hours. Just before serving, spoon fruit over Spanish Cream.

To Prepare in Advance: The Spanish Cream may be stored, covered, in the refrigerator for up to 48 hours. The Sangría Fruit is best served within 12 hours.

DINNER ON TRAYS
AT AN OUTDOOR CONCERT
(FOR 6)

*Chilled Champagne
with Fresh Berries*

---

*Individual Servings of Raw Vegetables
with Fresh Herb Dip*

Turkey, Snow Pea, and Red Pepper Salad Mangia

French Cheese and Crackers on an Ivy Leaf

Glazed Fruit Tart with Cream Cheese Filling

Thermos Coffee

DINNER ON TRAYS
AT AN OUTDOOR CONCERT

In the summers before air-conditioning was universal, when the sun began to set we would collectively move out of the house—onto the veranda, the patio, or, for lack of these, to take an evening stroll down the block. We just couldn't wait to get out into the balmy night air, with its fireflies and the hope of a cooling breeze. But if there was something more exciting to do on these languid evenings, we were up to it. An evening ball game, a harness race, a concert in the park—we could hardly wait to get there, and we took a picnic dinner with us, elaborate or modest, to be enjoyed in the grandstands before the crowd arrived or nibbled at all evening long. One thing about those evenings was certain: We were never hungrier, nor was eating ever more joyful.

As adults we still love to picnic on balmy evenings, and have discovered, along with a lot of others, that concert picnics have become almost a new art form. We have watched Hollywood Bowl revelers on opening night present elaborate international picnics to their guests, including 25-pound suckling pigs on silver trays and gloved houseboys pouring Champagne to guests dining on specially-designed folding tables. We prefer a slightly less formal presentation, a menu that can be served on lap trays.

Organization is the key, whether or not the picnic is to be elaborate. We suggest using stacking plastic trays and carrying two hampers, one for food, the other for the beverages. It is cocktail time upon arrival, and for this menu we like chilled Champagne poured over fresh or frozen berries. Berries are preferred for two reasons: First, they are unusual and festive, rising and falling in the glass with the bubbles, and second, we can use a less expensive Champagne, and consequently more of it. You wouldn't want to adulterate a first-quality wine with such a strong fruit flavor as boysenberries or blackberries. The wine keeps everyone chatting and busy as we, the hosts, begin the magic act of producing an outdoor feast. The beverage hamper now acts as a serving table for our stacking trays, which are completed, one by one, with all the courses except dessert. First we set out small dishes of cut raw vegetables with dip. Then we arrange the stunning salad of turkey, red bell peppers, and snow peas, with a dressing flavored with Chinese sesame oil, and we place wedges of cheese and crackers on ivy leaves. Now the trays are passed. There is plenty of time to dine and chat leisurely as the sun sets. Trays can be collected before the concert begins.

Dessert, a luscious glazed fruit tart topped with the most beautiful summer fruits found in the market this morning, is saved to serve with coffee during intermission. We suggest that you bring entirely too many tarts and share them with your neighbors. Who can tell? It may establish your reputation on the spot.

SHOPPING LIST

Fruits for tart (your choice)
3   medium-size red bell peppers
8   ounces Chinese snow peas or sugar snap peas
1   basket boysenberries, blackberries, or raspberries
1   bunch chives or a small bunch scallions
     Fresh tarragon or dill (1 tablespoon minced)
6   mint sprigs
1   lemon (for juice)
2   to 3 carrots, for curls
½   jicama
1   small fennel bulb or 1 celery heart
1   small head broccoli
6   mushrooms
1   basket cherry tomatoes
1   medium-size summer squash (zucchini, crookneck, or pattypan)

Turkey or chicken breast (to make 2½ cups cooked and cubed)
1   cup (8 ounces) sour cream
8   ounces cream cheese
½   cup (4 ounces) heavy cream
2   sticks butter
1   egg
8   ounces frozen boysenberries, blackberries, or raspberries (if fresh not available)
4   ounces jam or jelly (flavor depends on fruits chosen for tart)
⅓   cup pine nuts or slivered almonds
     Plain crackers
2   bottles Champagne

From a cheese shop

French cheese (your choice)

65

Staples

Mayonnaise (½ cup)
Safflower oil (⅓ cup)
Garlic (2 cloves)
Worcestershire sauce (¼ teaspoon)
Balsamic vinegar or Sherry vinegar (2 teaspoons)
Chinese sesame oil (2 to 3 teaspoons)

All-purpose flour (1¾ cups)
Sugar (about ½ cup)
Onion powder (½ teaspoon)
Brandy, Kirsch, dark rum, or Grand Marnier (1 tablespoon)
Vanilla (½ teaspoon)
Salt

DO-AHEAD TIMETABLE

Up to a month ahead: Freeze tart shell

Up to a week ahead: Make herb dip

Up to three days ahead: Cook turkey

Day of the party: Bake tart shell and cool. Chill Champagne. Arrange dipping vegetables in serving dishes. Blanch red peppers and snow peas for salad. Roast pine nuts. Cut up turkey. Fill and glaze tart. Fill Thermos with coffee

Just before leaving for the concert: Pack ice chests. Toss salad with dressing

Chilled Champagne with Fresh Berries

FOR 6 SERVINGS, WITH SECONDS

This combination has become our favorite summertime drink. Buy an inexpensive brand of Champagne.

1   basket boysenberries, blackberries, or raspberries, *or* 8 ounces frozen whole berries
1   magnum or 2 bottles Champagne, chilled

Place 3 or more berries in each stemmed glass. Fill glasses slowly with chilled Champagne, taking care berries don't spill over. Serve immediately.

Individual Servings of Raw Vegetables with Fresh Herb Dip

FOR 6 SERVINGS

Each tray has a small bowl of raw vegetables surrounding a container (in this case, an egg cup) of dip. For this menu we recommend a tarragon-flavored dip. Fresh tarragon leaves can be preserved indefinitely if covered with vinegar and refrigerated; squeeze out excess vinegar before use. The dip may take on other flavors by omitting the tarragon and adding any one of the following: 2 tablespoons fresh dill, 1½ teaspoons curry powder, 2 jars marinated artichoke hearts (drained and chopped), or 4 ounces caviar (rinsed and dried; garnish this with fresh lemon wheels).

RAW VEGETABLES (use an assortment of the following, keeping in mind a variety of colors and textures):

2	carrots, cut into spears or curls
½	jícama, cut into ½-inch spears
1	celery heart *or* 1 small fennel bulb (if available), cut into spears
1	small head broccoli, cut into florets
3 to 4	mushrooms, quartered lengthwise
1	medium-size summer squash (zucchini, crookneck, or pattypan), cut into thin diagonal slices
1	basket cherry tomatoes, with stems

FRESH HERB DIP (makes about 1½ cups):

1	cup sour cream
½	cup mayonnaise
2	scallions, finely chopped, *or* 1 tablespoon finely snipped fresh chives
1	tablespoon or more minced fresh tarragon (if not available, use fresh dill)
½	teaspoon onion powder
½	teaspoon Balsamic vinegar (see Note), optional

Note: Italian Balsamic vinegar is available in gourmet specialty shops and many supermarkets. It is dark, syrupy, and slightly sweet (from the natural sweetness of the grapes used in its making), and has a very mellow flavor from being aged, sometimes for many years, in vats made from different woods. The vinegar is expensive, but a little goes a long way.

Arrange the cut vegetables in serving dishes around a small container, such as an egg cup or ramekin.

Stir together the dip ingredients. At serving time, spoon into egg cups or small ramekins nestled among the cut vegetables.

To Prepare in Advance: Arrange vegetables in their serving dishes surrounding a small dish into which the dip can be spooned just before serving. Cover the vegetables with damp paper towels and place each in a separate plastic bag. Refrigerate up to 24 hours. The dip will keep a week in the refrigerator, but develops a stronger herb flavor as it stands.

Turkey, Snow Pea, and Red Pepper Salad Mangia

FOR 6 SERVINGS

The inspiration for this salad comes from a romantic lunch we enjoyed at Mangia, a Los Angeles restaurant serving Northern Italian cuisine.

2½   cups cooked turkey or chicken breast, cut into ¾-inch dice

3   medium-size red bell peppers, seeds and membranes removed, cut into ¾-inch squares

8   ounces fresh Chinese snow peas *or* sugar snap peas, strings removed

⅓   cup pine nuts *or* slivered almonds, sautéed in 2 teaspoons butter until evenly golden

DRESSING:

2   garlic cloves, peeled

3   tablespoons fresh lemon juice

> 2   teaspoons Balsamic vinegar *or* Sherry vinegar (see Note)
> ⅓   cup safflower oil *or* other light vegetable oil
> 2 to 3   teaspoons Chinese sesame oil, to taste
>   Salt to taste

Note: A description of Balsamic vinegar appears in the previous recipe. Sherry vinegar from France or Spain, often used by modern chefs, has a distinct, rich Sherry taste, and has often been aged 25 years or more.

Place the turkey in a medium-size salad bowl. To heighten the color and flavor of the red peppers and snow peas, steam them for 1 to 2 minutes, or blanch by dropping them into a large pot of rapidly boiling water for 30 to 45 seconds. Drain and immediately plunge into ice water to cool. Drain, blot dry with paper towels, and add to the bowl with the turkey.

To make the dressing, combine the ingredients in a food processor or blender and blend well. Pour the dressing over the salad ingredients and toss to coat evenly. Refrigerate for at least an hour or up to 6 hours.

Just before serving, arrange the salad on a platter and sprinkle with the toasted pine nuts or almonds.

To Prepare in Advance: The salad should be chilled for at least an hour for the flavors to mingle. If stored longer than 6 hours it loses its fresh appearance.

 *French Cheese and Crackers on an Ivy Leaf*

For this menu, we like to serve individual wedges of cheese and plain crackers on an ivy leaf (washed and dried). A good choice of cheese here would be *Bonchampi* mushroom cheese, or any other unusual creamy cheese.

 *Glazed Fruit Tart with Cream Cheese Filling*

MAKES A 9- TO 10-INCH TART SERVING 6 TO 8

When doing cooking demonstrations we enjoy using our easy cream cheese filling for tarts instead of the traditional custard known as *crème patissière* which takes much longer to make. The filling has an affinity for all types of summer fruits.

A 9- to 10-inch tart pan with removable bottom, lined with sweet tart pastry (recipe follows) and fully baked
Fresh fruit of your choice, washed, sliced if necessary (we recommend whole strawberries, raspberries, blueberries, or grapes; sliced peaches, nectarines, kiwis, or plums; or halved figs)

CREAM CHEESE FILLING:

8 ounces cream cheese
⅓ cup sugar
½ teaspoon vanilla
½ cup heavy cream, whipped

GLAZE:

½ cup jam or jelly of your choice (for light-colored fruits use apricot or apple; for dark fruits, use red currant or the flavor of the fruit you are using).
1 tablespoon brandy, Kirsch, dark rum, *or* Grand Marnier

TO GARNISH AND SERVE:

Sprigs of fresh mint

To make the filling, warm the cream cheese slightly: Either place it in a glass bowl and microwave at high power for 15 seconds or heat it in the top of a double boiler over hot water. When soft and creamy, stir in the sugar and vanilla. Cool slightly, then fold in the whipped cream. Set aside.

Dinner on Trays at an Outdoor Concert

Champagne with Boysenberries
Raw Vegetables with Fresh Herb Dip
French Cheeses
Turkey, Snow Pea and
Red Pepper Salad
Glazed Fruit Tart

If using jam for the glaze, puree it until smooth in a food processor or blender. Heat jam or jelly in a small saucepan until liquefied. Brush a thin layer over the inside of the cooled tart shell to "waterproof" the pastry. Add the flavoring of your choice to the remaining glaze and stir to combine.

Fill the tart shell with the cream cheese mixture, smoothing it to make an even layer. Stud the top of the tart completely with selected fruit. Brush or drizzle the glaze over the fruit. (If using fruits that darken on standing, be sure to cover them completely with glaze.) Garnish with mint sprigs. Chill for at least 30 minutes before cutting.

To Prepare in Advance: This is at its best the day it is made. Keep chilled until serving time.

 ## Sweet Tart Pastry (Pâte Sucrée)

FOR A 9- OR 10-INCH TART

This is the pastry we always use for tarts; it's quick, failure-proof, and delicious.

  1½ cups all-purpose flour
  10 tablespoons (1¼ sticks) chilled unsalted butter, cut into small cubes
   3 tablespoons sugar
  ⅛ teaspoon salt
   1 egg, lightly beaten

This can be made in a food processor or on a work table or board.

To make pastry in the processer, combine flour, butter, sugar, and salt in the container fitted with the steel blade. Process in on–off bursts until the the mixture looks like coarse cornmeal. With machine running, add the beaten egg slowly through the feed tube until the mixture just begins to form into a mass. Turn out onto waxed paper or plastic wrap and press into a disk.

To make the dough on a work table, place the flour in a mound. Make a well in the center and add the remaining ingredients. Work the dough with your fingers into a compact mass. Place the dough close to you and, using the heel of your hand, take a chunk about the size of a golf ball and smear it about 10 inches away from you, keeping your fingers pointed upward. Repeat the same movement, smearing more and more dough toward the first portion, until it has all been pushed away from you. Gather the dough into one mass and repeat the operation once or twice more until the dough is well-blended.

Preheat oven to 400°F.

Roll out the dough on a floured surface (we use a pastry cloth) to make an 11- to 12-inch circle. Line the tart pan, rolling the pin over the edge to trim the dough flush with the top edge of the pan. Since the pastry is crumbly, like a cookie dough, you may have to patch it a bit as you work.

To bake the tart shell, line the pastry with parchment or waxed paper and fill with raw beans, rice, or pie weights. Bake for 10 minutes. Remove the paper and weights, prick the bottom of the tart shell with a fork, and continue baking until golden brown, about 15 to 20 minutes longer. Remove from oven and cool.

To Prepare in Advance: The uncooked pastry may be made several days ahead of time and refrigerated if you do not used unbleached flour, which turns grey on standing. The dough also freezes for months.

A FAMILY REUNION IN THE PARK
(FOR 12 TO 16)

Chilled Beer, Soft Drinks, and Lemonade

*Basket of Raw Vegetables
with Cucumber Dip*

Crescent Moon Barbecued Beef Roast

Grilled Onions

Grilled Corn on the Cob

Roman Holiday Pasta Salad

Zucchini Relish

Fresh Fruit

Outrageous Oatmeal Cookies

A FAMILY REUNION IN THE PARK

Organize your family and get them to the park. We mean the whole family. Accept no excuses. Arrange transportation if you must. Tell Teddy it's okay to bring his dog. Ask Aunt Martha to bring her famous pickles—she'll come. Assign someone to bring the beer, someone the lemonade, someone else the folding tables and cloths. In short, get 'em outside and away from television. Have your own ball game, your own Olympics, anything. There may be some resistance at first, but once they're there, they're going to love it, and they'll possibly talk more than they have all year. And that's what families should do.

Pick a local park. Put up a big banner with your family's name on it. Tie balloons and streamers from the ends. You just might start a summer tradition.

Don't forget the camera!

SHOPPING LIST

10 medium zucchini
24 ears fresh corn
20 medium-size brown onions
4 medium-size red onions
2 red or green bell peppers (to hold dip—they should stand upright)
3 medium-size green bell peppers
1 medium-size red bell pepper
2 large ripe tomatoes
2 heads salad bowl or other curly lettuce
1 bunch small carrots with long, leafy tops (to decorate basket)
1 fresh parsley
   Assorted vegetables for dipping (8 ounces snow peas or sugar snap peas, 8 medium mushrooms, 1 zucchini, 1 basket cherry tomatoes, 1 small head cauliflower, 2 bunches scallions, 6 medium carrots, 6 celery stalks, 1 medium jícama)
2 large hothouse cucumbers
1 bunch scallions or chives
   Fresh oregano (2 tablespoons chopped)
1 bunch dill
3 lemons (for juice)
   Assorted fresh fruits for dessert
   A 5-pound eye of round or round beef roast
3 sticks butter

3 cups (1½ pounds) small-curd cottage cheese
¾ cup (6 ounces) sour cream
   Frozen lemonade mix
6 cups old-fashioned oats
2 packages (12 ounces each) shell or bow-shaped pasta
   Brown sugar (2 cups)
2 cups broken walnuts
6 ounces semisweet chocolate morsels
   Sweet or dill pickles (for 2 cups diced)
18 ounces white vinegar
1 jar (8 ounces) Dijon mustard
   Beer
   Soft drinks
   Ice

Staples

   Mayonnaise (1½ cups)
   Vegetable oil (1½ cups)
   Olive oil, extra-virgin (⅔ cup)
   Garlic (6 cloves)
   Eggs (2)
   Sugar (4 cups)
   Wholewheat flour (2 cups)
   Cornstarch (1 tablespoon)
   Tabasco sauce
   Celery salt (2 teaspoons)
   Dried dillweed (1½ teaspoons, if fresh not available)
   Dried oregano (2 teaspoons, if fresh not available)
   Whole or ground nutmeg (2 teaspoons)
   Dry mustard (1 tablespoon)

Turmeric (2 teaspoons)
Red pepper flakes (1 teaspoon)
Cracked black pepper (2
    teaspoons)
Salt (6 to 7 tablespoons)

From a variety store

⅔-yard-wide gingham ribbon,
    to decorate basket

DO-AHEAD TIMETABLE

Up to a month ahead: Make zucchini relish. Make cookies and freeze

Up to three days ahead: Prepare pasta salad except for final garnish. Make
    cucumber dip. Marinate beef roast

Up to two days ahead: Barbecue beef roast

One day ahead: Wrap corn for grilling. Cut vegetables for dipping. Thaw
    cookies

Day of the party: Cut bell peppers to hold dip. Chill beer, soft drinks, and
    lemonade

Just before leaving for picnic: Pack ice chests

Just before serving: Line basket with lettuce to hold vegetables and dip

Basket of Raw Vegetables with Cucumber Dip

FOR 16 OR MORE SERVINGS

This is always spectacular looking, especially when red bell peppers are available to hold the dip. You may wish to add a second dip, such as our Fresh Herb or Green Chile versions (see Index).

      Large shallow wicker basket with handle
2 heads salad bowl or other curly lettuce to line the basket
1 bunch small carrots with leafy tops to decorate the handle
      String or twist-ties seals
      A few sprigs of parsley
⅔ yard wide gingham ribbon for bow

RAW VEGETABLES (amount depends on how large a variety you choose):

8   ounces snow peas *or* sugar snap peas
8   medium mushrooms, quartered lengthwise
1   zucchini, sliced diagonally
1   basket cherry tomatoes
1   small head cauliflower, core removed, separated into florets
2   bunches scallions
6   medium carrots, cut into diagonal slices
6   celery stalks, cut into sticks
1   medium jícama, peeled and cut into sticks

CUCUMBER DIP (makes about 4 cups):

2   large hothouse cucumbers, seeded
3   cups small-curd cottage cheese
3   scallions, finely chopped *or* 2 tablespoons finely snipped fresh
        chives
1   large garlic clove, minced or pressed
    Salt
    Tabasco to taste

2   red or green bell peppers, tops removed, hollowed, and
        notched around the cut edge to make containers for
        the dip(s)

To prepare the basket, line it with crisp, fresh lettuce leaves and arrange the prepared vegetables on the lettuce.

To decorate the basket, fasten the bunch of carrots to the handle with string or twist-ties. Cover fastenings with parsley; tie in place with ribbon bow.

To make the dip, grate the cucumber with skin. Place it in a medium bowl with 1 teaspoon salt; let stand 10 to 15 minutes. Place half the shredded cucumber in a clean kitchen towel and squeeze out all excess moisture. Repeat with the remaining cucumber. Stir together the remaining ingredients, then mix in the cucumber. Season to taste with salt and Tabasco. Spoon the dip into the bell pepper cups and nestle among the cut vegetables. Store extra dip in refrigerator containers for refilling the peppers at the picnic site.

To Prepare in Advance: Wrap cut vegetables in damp paper towels and refrigerate in plastic bags up to 24 hours. The dip will keep for 3 to 4 days in the refrigerator.

 # Crescent Moon Barbecued Beef Roast

FOR 12 TO 16 SERVINGS

Our friend, Henri Schley, barbecued for us one summer evening during a crescent moon and shared his marinade recipe with us. The roast tastes even better the next day, so it can be cooked at home the day before the picnic, then easily sliced and served at the picnic site. If you opt for the do-ahead method, omit the grilled onions and corn on the cob, replacing them with Fiesta Corn Salad (see Index), so no cooking need be done at the site.

A 5-pound eye of round *or* round beef roast
2 garlic cloves, peeled and slivered
2 tablespoons chopped fresh oregano *or* 2 teaspoons dried
     oregano, crumbled
1 teaspoon red pepper flakes, crushed
Juice of 2 to 3 lemons
2 teaspoons cracked black pepper, or more to taste

Make incisions about ½ inch deep and 1 inch apart all over the roast and insert the slivers of garlic. Sprinkle with oregano and red pepper flakes. Place in a heavy-duty plastic bag with the lemon juice and marinate for at least 24 hours in the refrigerator.

Roast over greyed barbecue coals (Henri uses mesquite or grapevine wood) for about an hour, turning to cook evenly, until a thermometer inserted in the thickest part of the meat registers 130°F for rare.

Remove and test for doneness, and cook slightly longer if necessary. Sprinkle with cracked black pepper. Let rest for at least 15 minutes before slicing thinly to serve.

To Prepare in Advance: This is especially tender if cooked the day before serving. Cool, then refrigerate in a heavy plastic bag for up to 2 days. Leftovers freeze well for another occasion.

Grilled Onions

FOR 16 SERVINGS

Whole onions cooked in their skins become sweet and tender, with an indescribable smoky flavor.

16 medium-size brown onions

Onions may be left whole or halved. Place them on a grill over hot coals for 15 minutes, or until they have blackened on the outside and are soft inside. Serve hot, to be skinned and eaten with knife and fork.

Grilled Corn on the Cob

FOR 12 TO 16 SERVINGS

Foil-wrapped corn steams in butter and its own juices.

24   ears fresh corn, husks and silk removed
1½   cups (3 sticks) butter, softened
       Salt and freshly ground black pepper

Place the corn on individual double-layer squares of aluminum foil. Combine butter with salt and pepper to taste and spread about 1 tablespoon of the mixture over each ear of corn. Wrap securely.

Grill 6 to 8 inches from the coals for about 15 minutes, turning frequently. Open one package to test for doneness (corn will be tender when a kernel is pierced), and cook a few minutes longer if necessary. Serve right in the foil wrapper.

To Prepare in Advance: Season and wrap the corn the day before and refrigerate overnight.

Roman Holiday Pasta Salad

FOR 12 TO 16 SERVINGS

This is a beautiful make-ahead salad for all kinds of entertaining.

2   packages (12 ounces each) small *conchiglie* (shell) or *far-falline* (bow-tie) pasta
⅔   cup olive oil (extra-virgin preferred)
1 to 2   tablespoon fresh lemon juice
2   medium garlic cloves, minced or pressed
1   bunch dill (feathery leaves only) chopped, *or* 1½ teaspoons dried dillweed
2   teaspoons salt
½   teaspoon freshly ground black pepper
2   medium-size red onions, finely diced
2   medium-size green bell peppers, finely diced
2   large ripe tomatoes, seeded and finely diced
2   cups sweet or dill pickles, diced

Cook the pasta according to package directions. When just *al dente,* drain and rinse with cold water to stop the cooking. Drain well. Place in a large mixing bowl and toss with the olive oil, lemon juice, garlic, dill, salt, and pepper.

Reserve about ¼ of the onions, bell peppers, and tomatoes to use later to decorate the top of the salad. Fold the remaining vegetables and pickles into the pasta mixture. Taste for seasoning, adding more salt or pepper as needed.

Mound the salad in a serving bowl. Arrange the reserved onion, tomato and pepper in alternating circles on top of the salad. If desired, sprinkle the top of the salad with extra fresh or dried dill.

To Prepare in Advance: Make the salad at least 3 hours before serving to allow the flavors to develop fully. It may be stored, covered, in the refrigerator for up to 4 days.

Zucchini Relish

MAKES 7 TO 8 PINTS

If you are the beneficiary of great quantities of zucchini from your garden, or your neighbor's, you will especially appreciate this wonderful relish. It is delicious with barbecued roasts and hamburgers, and it makes a great year-round food gift.

10	medium zucchini, to make 10 cups finely shredded
4	medium onions, minced
1	medium-size green bell pepper, finely chopped
1	medium-size red bell pepper, finely chopped
5	tablespoons salt
2¼	cups cider vinegar
4	cups sugar
1	tablespoon dry mustard
2	teaspoons celery salt
2	teaspoons ground nutmeg
2	teaspoons turmeric
½	teaspoon freshly ground black pepper
1	tablespoon cornstarch, mixed to a paste with 2 tablespoons cold water
1	jar (8 ounces) Dijon mustard

Combine zucchini, onions, peppers, and salt in a large glass or stainless steel bowl and mix well. Cover with a towel and let stand overnight at room temperature. Drain and rinse vegetables in cold water. Drain well and place in a large stainless steel or enamel kettle with all remaining ingredients except the cornstarch and mustard. Bring to a boil and simmer uncovered, stirring often, for 30 minutes. Add the cornstarch mixture and simmer briefly until thickened. Stir in the mustard and remove from heat. Cool.

We usually ladle this into gift jars and store it in the refrigerator to avoid the rather tedious process involved in putting it up in sterilized jars. If you prefer to seal it in jars, ladle the *boiling* relish into 7 or 8 sterilized pint jars. Cover with sterilized lids and process 5 minutes according to jar manufacturer's directions.

To Prepare in Advance: This will keep indefinitely in the refrigerator. If sealed and processed in canning jars and stored in a cool, dark place, it will keep without losing flavor or color for 6 months without refrigeration.

 *Outrageous Oatmeal Cookies*

FOR 2 DOZEN COOKIES

These truly are outrageous—large, chewy, and wonderfully wholesome. Barbara Olsen, who grew up on these and shared her secret recipe, urges us to play with ingredients when making them, to try various flours, and even to substitute granola for some of the oatmeal in one batch.

1½	cups vegetable oil
2	eggs
2	cups whole wheat flour (or blends of other flours—see Note)
2	teaspoons baking powder
1	teaspoon salt
2	cups packed brown sugar (light or dark)
6	cups old-fashioned oats (or can use part granola)
2	cups broken walnuts
1	package (6 ounces) semi-sweet chocolate morsels
	about ½ cup warm water

Note: Barbara likes to experiment with a variety of flours from the health food store, substituting them for a portion of the whole wheat flour. She says ¼ cup of garbanzo bean flour gives a nutty flavor, and also recommends soy flour and wheat germ.

Preheat oven to 375⁰F and place rack in center position.

In a 4 cup measure combine the oil and egg and whisk briefly to combine. Combine the flour, baking powder, and salt in a very large mixing bowl and stir until blended. Add the remaining ingredients except water, and stir to combine. Add the oil and egg and work the dough with a wooden spoon until

moistened throughout—it will be very stiff. Add just enough warm water to make the mixture damp enough to hold together.

Generously grease a heavy baking sheet. Form the mixture with your fingers into mounds of about ⅓ cup each and place 3 inches apart on the prepared sheet. Bake for 12 to 15 minutes until a cookie feels done when pressed with a finger—do not overcook or try to brown them.

Cool briefy, then use a metal spatula to remove from baking sheet. Cool completely.

To Prepare in Advance: Store in an airtight container at room temperature for up to 3 days, or freeze for up to 3 months.

LUNCH IN AN OPEN MEADOW
(FOR 4)

Chilled Champagne

Fruity Chicken Salad
in Pineapple or Cantaloupe Shells

Cheese Wedges and Crackers

Apricot Bread

LUNCH IN AN OPEN MEADOW

What if we found ourselves in the middle of a huge meadow under a canopy of hundreds of colorful, hissing airbags, tethered by thick ropes or cables? We might feel as if we were playing in some friendly giant's tulip garden. But more likely it would be a rendezvous of ballooners in celebration of the two brothers Montgolfier, Jacques and Joseph, who on June 5, 1783, outside Annonay, France, inflated a paper balloon with hot air and began the age of flight.

If we ever attend such a lofty gathering, this is the menu we would prepare, to eat in the sky or on blankets on the ground as we watch the spectacle. After a surprising roar or two from neighboring gas burners it's high time for a glass of chilled Champagne, the traditional drink for such occasions. Not all the balloons launch at the same time, and in awaiting the scheduled ascent one can chat, examine, and marvel at the Disney-like beauty of this fantasy world. The huge bags filled with hot air, referred to as envelopes, come in every color and combination of colors, with gorgeous graphics of eagles, Greek goddesses, or flowers, and with panels proudly displaying their "N" numbers, similar to the numbers on a plane's wing by which it can be identified from the ground. We imagine one almost feels the need to lie down and look up. A stiff neck could ruin the day here.

It is soon time to be off, so all aboard into the wicker basket. The picnic equipment, more Champagne, the sweaters, and, oh yes, the binoculars.

Someone pulls the dragon's tail, it roars forth its fire once more, and we slowly begin to rise. We drift slowly into a hollow silence, with perhaps the faintest whisper of wind in the basketwork, interrupted occasionally by a far-off church bell or the chatter of passing birds. Our extraordinary lunch would consist of a lime- and sesame-dressed chicken salad studded with fruits of the season and served in half a fresh pineapple or cantaloupe, a moist and nutty apricot bread, and some cheese and crackers.

It would all be so delicious, this ballooning business.

SHOPPING LIST

2 small ripe pineapples or 2 medium-size ripe cantaloupes
1 medium papaya
1 basket strawberries
Raspberries, to garnish (optional)
1 bunch scallions
1 kiwi
1 orange (for grated rind)
1 lemon (for grated rind)
2 limes (for 3 tablespoons juice)
Chicken or turkey (to make 3 cups cooked and shredded)
1 egg
1 cup (8 ounces) small-curd cottage cheese
1 stick butter
6-ounce wedge of fine-quality Cheddar cheese
6 ounces *triple-crème* cheese (Explorateur, Boursault, Saint André, or Brie)
6 ounces Roquefort, Gorgonzola, or other blue-veined cheese
Carr's Water Biscuits or other unseasoned crackers to serve with cheese
¼ cup slivered almonds or walnut pieces
6 ounces dried apricots
1 cup chopped walnuts or pecans
2 bottles Champagne

Staples

All-purpose flour (1¼ cups)
Sesame seed (2 teaspoons)
Sugar (2 teaspoons)
Light brown sugar (½ cup firmly packed)
Baking powder (1½ teaspoons)
Baking soda (½ teaspoon)
Dry mustard (¼ teaspoon)
Salt

DO-AHEAD TIMETABLE

Up to a month ahead: Make and freeze apricot bread

Up to three days ahead: Cook chicken or turkey

Two days ahead: Wrap cheeses and crackers

Day of the party: Chill Champagne

Just before leaving for picnic: Assemble salad ingredients. Pack ice chests

Fruity Chicken Salad in Pineapple or Cantaloupe Shells

FOR 4 SERVINGS

Pineapples or cantaloupes serve as edible containers for chicken salad, dressed with an intriguing nutty-flavored sesame and lime dressing.

2   small ripe pineapples *or* 2 medium-size ripe cantaloupes
3   cups shredded cooked chicken or turkey meat
¼   cup toasted slivered almonds or walnut pieces
4   strawberries, sliced
1   medium-size ripe papaya, pitted, peeled, and diced

THE DRESSING:

3   scallions, including part of the green tops, coarsely chopped
3   tablespoons fresh lime juice
2   teaspoons sugar
¼   teaspoon dry mustard
⅓   cup vegetable oil
2   teaspoons toasted sesame seeds

TO GARNISH:

Fresh strawberries *or* raspberries
1   kiwi, peeled and sliced

If using pineapples for serving the salad, cut them in half lengthwise right through the crowns. Using a sharp paring knife or a grapefruit knife, cut the fruit out of the pineapple halves, leaving a ½- to ¾-inch shell. Turn the shells over to drain off any excess juice. Remove the core from the fruit you took out of the shell and discard it. Cut the remaining fruit into ¾-inch chunks and set aside.

If using cantaloupe, cut in half and remove the seeds. Hollow the melon in the same manner, but leave a 1-inch shell, and cut the remaining fruit into ¾-inch chunks.

Combine the chicken, nuts, strawberries, papaya, and pineapple or cantaloupe cubes in a mixing bowl; set aside. For dressing, combine scallions, lime juice, sugar, and mustard in a food processor or blender and process for about 10 to 15 seconds, until the onion is minced. With the motor running, slowly pour in the oil and blend until the mixture has thickened slightly. Add sesame seed and blend a few seconds longer. Pour over the salad mixture and toss lightly. Mound in the prepared pineapples or cantaloupes. Garnish each serving with fresh strawberries (halved if large) or raspberries, and slices of kiwi.

To Prepare in Advance: Assemble the salad within 8 hours of serving. The chicken or turkey may be cooked several days ahead.

Cheese Wedges and Crackers

FOR 4 SERVINGS

6 ounces Cheddar cheese
6 ounces *triple-crème* cheese, such as Explorateur, Boursault, Saint André, or Brie (plain, peppered, or herbed)
6 ounces Roquefort, Gorgonzola, *or* other blue-veined cheese
 Carr's Water Biscuits *or* other unseasoned crackers of your choice

Cut cheeses into fourths (1½ ounce portions) and wrap airtight in plastic. Wrap crackers, 8 to a package. Pack cheese and crackers in a noncrushable container and keep in a cool place. Cheeses are best served at room temperature.

To Prepare in Advance: Wrap cheeses and crackers up to 48 hours in advance. Keep the cheese chilled until about 2 hours before serving.

Apricot Bread

MAKES ONE 9x5-INCH LOAF

This wholesome and delicious bread derives its moistness from the addition of cottage cheese.

Butter and flour for pan
¼ cup (½ stick) butter
½ cup firmly packed light brown sugar
1 teaspoon each grated lemon and orange rind
1 egg
1 cup small-curd cottage cheese
1¼ cups all-purpose flour
1½ teaspoons baking powder
½ teaspoon baking soda
½ teaspoon salt
1 cup (6 ounces) chopped dried apricots
1 cup chopped walnuts or pecans
1 tablespoon butter, melted

Butter and flour a 9x5-inch loaf pan. Adjust rack to center of oven and preheat the oven to 350°F (325°F if using a glass pan).

In a large mixing bowl, beat together the butter, brown sugar, and lemon and orange rinds until creamy. Add the egg and cottage cheese and beat well, scraping the sides of the bowl from time to time.

In another bowl stir together the flour, baking powder, soda, salt, apricots, and nuts.

Stir the flour mixture into the butter mixture until well blended; the mixture will be very stiff. Press into the prepared loaf pan, smoothing the top with a spatula or dampened fingers. Brush the top of the loaf with 1 tablespoon melted butter.

Bake until a toothpick inserted in the center of the bread comes out clean, about 40 to 45 minutes (50 minutes for glass pan). Cool on a rack in the pan for 10 minutes, then turn out of the pan to cool thoroughly.

To Prepare in Advance: When cool, wrap the bread airtight in foil or plastic wrap. It may be stored in the refrigerator for up to a week, or in the freezer for up to 3 months.

FRENCH PICNIC FARE
(Déjeuner sur l'Herbe)
(FOR 6)

Kir

Chicken Liver Pâté Maison in Crusty French Baguettes

Beaujolais or Red Burgundy

Mustard-Glazed Rock Cornish Game Hens

Red Pepper Quiche

*French Potato Salad
with Wine and Herb Dressing*

Matisse Fruit Basket

French Triple-Crème Cheeses

FRENCH PICNIC FARE

There is a park in Paris called the Bois de Boulogne that has acquired the nickname of the "playground of Paris." This park, a favorite pleasure ground since the 17th century, encloses beautiful promenades, bridle paths, lakes, and race courses, including the famous Longchamps. For those who live in a city, a well-attended park with its bowers, secluded gardens, and ponds can be a convenient and ideal spot for a gourmet getaway picnic. In no time at all, after stopping at *boulangeries, pâtisseries, charcuteries,* and a favorite wine merchant, one can assemble a magnificent *déjeuner sur l'herbe* (lunch on the grass).

Before we were married we courted in Paris, and we have a treasury of memories of that time. Recreating the feeling of those days has become a favorite pastime of ours during the summer, when parks are at their most beautiful and there are friends with whom we wish to spend a leisurely afternoon.

The festivities begin with Kir, an aperitif of chilled white wine and blackcurrant liqueur, accompanied by slices of velvety pâté encased in crusty French bread.

For the main course we have an array of French country dishes. Cornish game hens have been split and marinated in mustard and garlic and broiled, so they are easy to eat with the fingers. The same Dijon mustard flavors French Potato Salad, which, unlike the typical American sour cream- and mayonnaise-dressed mixture, is made from potatoes which are marinated in broth and wine when still warm from cooking, then lightly dressed with herbed oil and vinegar. Quiches have become a bit *démodé,* but we agree with our friend Jacques Pépin, author of a number of books on French cooking, that when properly done, quiches will always be wonderful. Ours has an exceptionally sturdy crust, flavored with olive oil, that will hold up well during transport to the park. The filling is an herb-flavored custard laced with strips of red and green bell peppers and leeks. With the main course we will enjoy a French Beaujolais, for few wines taste so wonderful with French food. Unlike most red wines, this is usually drunk young (many Frenchmen prefer it only months old), and served chilled.

Dessert reminds us of an impressionist's still life. It's an arrangement of the most choice fruit in the market—wedges of icy watermelon, grapes, peaches, figs, plums, pears, and apricots. This is accompanied by a variety of some extraordinary French cheeses to spread on crusty bread, fresh this morning from a local bakery.

The casual charm of this menu will inspire relaxed conversation long into a summer afternoon.

SHOPPING LIST

2 pounds medium-size red potatoes
2 medium leeks or 1 medium onion
1 large shallot or 3 scallions
2 medium-size red bell peppers
1 bunch basil or tarragon
1 bunch dill
Fresh parsley
1 lemon or orange (for rind, to garnish drinks)
¼ watermelon
1 pound seedless green grapes
1 pound seedless red grapes
3 freestone peaches
3 apricots
6 fresh figs
3 plums
3 pears
3 rock Cornish game hens (about 22 ounces each)
8 ounces chicken livers
10 to 12 ounces assorted wedges of *triple-crème* cheeses (Explorateur, Boursault, Brie, Saint André, etc.)

6 ounces Swiss cheese
Parmesan cheese (for ¼ cup grated)
5 eggs
3 sticks unsalted butter
1½ cups (12 ounces) half and half or light cream
2 cups cake flour
1 long, narrow French bread baguette
Carr's Water Biscuits, Bremner Wafers, or other unseasoned crackers to serve with cheese
1 cup olive oil
2 bottles (750 ml each) Beaujolais or red Burgundy
2 bottles (750 ml each) dry white wine (such as Chablis or French Colombard)
½ cup *crème de cassis* (black currant liqueur)
3 tablespoons Port
3 tablespoons dry vermouth or white wine

Staples

    Garlic (2 cloves)

    Chicken broth (3 tablespoons)

    Red wine vinegar (about ⅓ cup)

    Dijon mustard (about 2½ tablespoons)

    Worcestershire sauce (1 teaspoon)

    Dried dillweed (½ to ¾ teaspoon, if fresh not available)

    Dried basil or tarragon (¾ teaspoon, if fresh not available)

    Dry mustard (2 teaspoons)

    Paprika (½ teaspoon)

    Ground allspice (⅛ teaspoon)

    Whole nutmeg (⅛ teaspoon freshly grated)

    Cayenne pepper (⅛ teaspoon)

    Salt

    Black pepper

From the garden, nursery or florist

    Nontoxic flowers, such as nasturtiums, to garnish the fruit basket.

    Garden leaves, such as ivy, grape, citrus, etc.

DO-AHEAD TIMETABLE

Up to a month ahead: Freeze pâté in French bread. Freeze crust for quiche

Up to three days ahead: Make potato salad. Make pâté in French bread (if not frozen)

Two days ahead: Wrap cheeses

One day ahead: Cook game hens. Thaw pâté in French bread

Day of the party: Bake crust; fill and bake quiche. Chill white wine

Just before leaving for picnic: Bring game hens to room temperature. Pack ice chests

During the party: Open red wine. Assemble fruit bowl

Kir

FOR 6 SINGLE SERVINGS

Serve this aperitif with the Pâté in Baguettes. It is named for Canon Kir, onetime mayor of Dijon, France, who was famous for ordering this very pleasant drink. *Crème de cassis* is a black currant syrup or liqueur, available at liquor stores.

   1   bottle (750 ml) chilled dry white wine (such as Chablis or
          French Colombard)
  ¼   cup (2 ounces) *crème de cassis*
   6   strips of lemon peel

Pour the wine into the glasses, followed by 2 teaspoons *crème de cassis* (the latter will sink to the bottom). Drop a strip of lemon peel into each and serve.

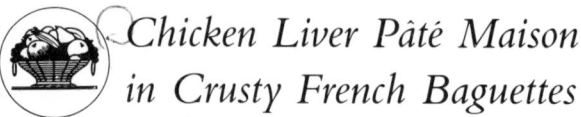

Chicken Liver Pâté Maison
in Crusty French Baguettes

MAKES 1½ CUPS PATE, TO FILL 1 LOAF OF FRENCH BREAD

This is the quickest pâté we've yet devised, and the easiest to serve, as no spreading is required.

   8   ounces chicken livers, rinsed and dried
   1   large shallot *or* the white part of 3 scallions
   2   teaspoons dry mustard
   1   teaspoon salt
  ⅛   teaspoon ground allspice
  ⅛   teaspoon freshly grated nutmeg
  ⅛   teaspoon cayenne pepper

3   tablespoons Port
1   cup (2 sticks) unsalted butter, at room temperature
1   tablespoon minced fresh parsley

TO SERVE:

1   long, narrow loaf (baguette) of French bread

Place the chicken livers in a small saucepan and cover with cold water. Bring to a boil, then lower the heat and simmer slowly for 10 minutes.

Meanwhile, mince the shallot or scallions in a blender or food processor fitted with the steel blade. Add the seasonings.

When the chicken livers have cooked, drain them well and add them to the blender or food processor. Process to a smooth paste, then add the Port and continue processing, stopping the motor from time to time to scrape down the sides of the container with a rubber spatula. Let cool to room temperature. Add the butter about ½ stick at a time, processing until very smooth and scraping the sides of the container often. Add the minced parsley and process briefly to mix.

Cut the loaf of French bread in half crosswise and cut off the ends. Using your fingers or a grapefruit knife, remove the soft bread interior from each piece (save it for another purpose, such as poultry stuffings), leaving a hollow shell of crisp crust. Cover one end of each bread "tube" with plastic wrap, held in place with a rubber band. Spoon the pâté into the two tubes, tapping it lightly to remove any air bubbles that may form and filling to the top. Cover the filled bread crusts with plastic wrap and place upright in the refrigerator to chill until the pâté has firmed. When cold, remove rubber bands and wrap airtight in foil.

To serve, use a serrated slicing knife to cut crosswise into ¼- to ½-inch slices.

To Prepare in Advance: Store up to 3 days in the refrigerator or 2 months in the freezer. Thaw for an hour or two at room temperature before slicing.

Mustard-Glazed Rock Cornish Game Hens

FOR 6 SERVINGS

The mustardy marinade which flavors these hens is also excellent on chicken that is to be broiled or charcoal-grilled.

MARINADE:

4   teaspoons Dijon mustard
1   small garlic clove, minced or pressed
¼   cup red wine vinegar
1   tablespoon minced fresh parsley
1   teaspoon Worcestershire sauce
½   teaspoon paprika
¼   cup olive oil

3   rock Cornish game hens (22 ounces each), thawed (see Note)

Note: To save some time, ask your butcher to saw the frozen hens in half for you.

To make the marinade, combine the mustard and garlic in a small mixing bowl. Whisk in the vinegar, parsley, Worcestershire, and paprika. Gradually add the olive oil, whisking constantly until the dressing is smooth and emulsified.

Using poultry shears, split the game hens in half along the backbone and breastbone, removing the backbone completely. (Save the backbone and giblets for stock.) Arrange the halved hens skin side down in a foil-lined broiler pan. Pour the marinade over them, cover, and leave at room temperature for 1 hour. Drain off the marinade and reserve it.

Preheat the broiler. Broil the hens at least 6 inches from the heat source for 15 minutes. Turn the hens skin side up and broil for 10 to 15 minutes longer, brushing once or twice with the reserved marinade. Cool and refrigerate.

To Prepare in Advance: Cook the hens 1 to 2 days before serving and store, covered, in the refrigerator. These taste best when not overly chilled, so let them approach room temperature before serving.

Red Pepper Quiche

FOR 6 TO 8 SERVINGS

The olive oil pastry, adapted from a country French recipe by Richard Olney, makes a sturdy crust that is extremely moisture-resistant and travels well. If you have another favorite pastry, though, you can use it instead if you wish.

OLIVE OIL PASTRY:

2	cups cake flour
1	teaspoon salt
1	egg
⅓	cup olive oil

FILLING:

2	medium leeks *or* 1 medium onion
3	tablespoons butter
1	small garlic clove, minced or pressed
2	medium-size red bell peppers, seeds and membranes removed, cut into julienne strips
¼	cup freshly grated Parmesan cheese
6	ounces Swiss cheese, shredded
4	eggs
1½	cups half and half or light cream
2	tablespoons minced fresh parsley
2	teaspoons minced fresh herbs, such as basil, tarragon, or dill, *or* ¾ teaspoon dried herbs, crumbled
½	teaspoon salt
	generous pinch of cayenne pepper
1	tablespoon butter, melted

To prepare the crust, place flour and salt in a bowl or in food processor fitted with the steel blade. Whisk together the egg and olive oil and mix into the flour; the dough will be soft. Turn out onto plastic wrap and form into disc; wrap airtight. Let rest at room temperature for 1 hour. Place on a well-floured surface (we use a pastry cloth) and roll out into a 13-inch circle (it will be quite thin). Use the dough to line a 10- or 11-inch quiche dish or tart pan. Trim crust to 1 inch above edge of pan, and crimp the edges decoratively above the rim of the pan.

Preheat oven to 450°F. While preparing the filling, partially bake the pastry for 10 minutes. To prepare the leeks, trim away the root end and most of the green. Cut in half lengthwise, then rinse well under cold running water separating the layers. Cut into ¼-inch crosswise slices. If using an onion, mince. Sauté leeks or onion in a medium skillet in 2 tablespoons of the butter until soft but not browned. Add the garlic and sauté briefly. Turn out of pan and set aside. Melt the remaining 1 tablespoon butter in the same skillet over high heat and sauté the red peppers very quickly until slightly browned and blistered. Sprinkle the bottom of the crust with the Parmesan and arrange the shredded Swiss evenly over it. Top the cheese with a layer of leeks or onions, then peppers.

Whisk together the eggs, cream, parsley, herbs, and seasonings and pour this custard over the ingredients in the crust. Bake at 350°F for 45 minutes. Remove from oven and brush crust with melted butter to glaze and soften it. Allow to rest at room temperature for at least 10 minutes before cutting.

To Prepare in Advance: Cool the quiche on a rack at room temperature; the filling will toughen if refrigerated. It may be reheated at 350°F for 10 to 15 minutes.

 *French Potato Salad with Wine and Herb Dressing*

FOR 6 TO 8 SERVINGS

Dressed in wine and an herb vinaigrette, this is lighter and more delicate than most potato salads. Use fresh dill, if available; its special flavor makes all the difference.

6 to 8   medium-size red potatoes (2 pounds)
3   tablespoons dry vermouth or white wine
3   tablespoons chicken broth

WINE AND HERB DRESSING:

1 large shallot, minced
1 medium garlic clove, minced
1 tablespoon Dijon mustard
1½ tablespoons wine vinegar
2 to 3 teaspoons snipped fresh dill, *or* ½ to ¾ teaspoon dried
dried dillweed
¼ cup olive oil
Freshly ground black pepper

TO GARNISH AND SERVE:

Sprigs of fresh dill

Scrub the potatoes and place them in a large saucepan with cold water to cover. Bring to a boil, then lower the heat and simmer for about 20 minutes, or until they are tender when pierced with a sharp knife. Drain and let stand just until cool enough to handle. You may peel the potatoes or not, as you choose (we don't). Cut into ¼-inch slices and drop them into a mixing bowl. Pour the wine and broth over them while they are warm, and let stand while you make the dressing.

In a small mixing bowl, combine the shallot and garlic with the mustard, vinegar, and dill. Whisking constantly, pour in the oil in a slow, steady stream. Pour the dressing over the potatoes and toss gently. Arrange on a serving dish and sprinkle with pepper. Garnish with sprigs of fresh dill. Serve warm or at room temperature.

To Prepare in Advance: The flavor of this salad is at its best when freshly made, though it may be refrigerated for up to 4 days. Bring to room temperature before serving.

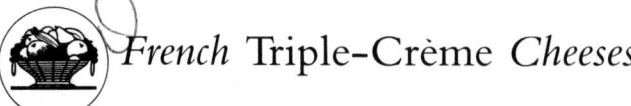French Triple-Crème Cheeses

Triple-crème cheeses are rich and luxurious. Some of those that we particularly enjoy are Explorateur, Boursault, Saint André, and Brillat Savarin, found in most cheese shops. Serve them with simple crackers such as Carr's Water Biscuits or Bremner Wafers.

Matisse Fruit Basket

FOR 6 SERVINGS

A fruit arrangement that looks as if it were lifted from a Matisse canvas serves as both centerpiece and finale to your French picnic.

	A round wicker basket, approximately 12 inches in diameter
	About 12 assorted grape or ivy leaves, washed
¼	watermelon, cut lengthwise
1	pound each green and red seedless grapes
3	peaches (freestone, not cling)
3	apricots
6	figs
3	plums
3	pears
	Fresh nontoxic flowers, such as nasturtiums, for decoration

Line the basket with most of the leaves. Arrange the fruit attractively in the basket, cutting the watermelon into 2 wedges. Insert extra leaves where needed to balance the arrangement.

A SIMPLE MENU FOR A DAY AT SEA
(FOR 6)

Iced Jasmine Tea and Chilled Mineral Water

Curried Rice Salad with Ham and Peaches

Fresh Figs and Cherries

Cheese Wedges and Crackers

Rocky Road Clusters

A Simple Menu for a Day at Sea

All of our senses expand on the water. The sun seems brighter, there is more sky above us, and the light reflected by the changing waves attacks us from all angles. The movement of the water tests our sense of balance. Perhaps sounds are the most noticeably different. You can actually hear faraway noises in stereo, punctuated by the screech of seagulls. Perhaps it's lost foghorns, or whispering city noises, but certainly you hear the constant rush and rhythmic slapping of water on the hull. It's not surprising that people run away to sea and pay huge sums for ocean voyages; it's medicine for the mind. It is difficult to know what to credit—the air, the motion, the sun—perhaps all of these, but one thing is sure. After a bit of this tonic, you sleep better and eat better.

Boating requires a lot of food and a lot of liquids, because appetites for both are magnified outdoors; however, we've discovered that the sun doesn't mix well with liquor. We recommend soft drinks—iced tea or chilled mineral water.

Food should be satisfying and simple to serve. Fresh peaches add both color and flavor to a superb chicken salad dressed with a curry and chutney dressing. There are also individually-wrapped wedges of cheese and crackers and some chocolate confections for nibbling any time.

SHOPPING LIST

	Cherries
	Fresh figs
8 to 10	peaches
4	celery stalks
2	bunches scallions (¾ cup sliced)
1	pound cooked ham
12	ounces or more assorted cheeses (Cheddar, Swiss, dill-flavored Havarti)
½	cup (4 ounces) sour cream
1½	cups converted rice
	Crackers to serve with cheese

	Jasmine tea
12	ounces semisweet chocolate morsels
12	regular marshmallows
½	cup crunchy peanut butter
¾	cup raisins
¼	cup mango chutney
	Mineral water

Staples

Mayonnaise (½ cup)

Curry powder (1½ teaspoons)

DO-AHEAD TIMETABLE

Up to three days ahead: Make confections

Two days ahead: Wrap cheeses and crackers

One day ahead: Make salad

Day of the party: Make iced tea

Just before leaving for picnic: Pack ice chests

 *Curried Rice Salad with Ham and Peaches*

FOR 6 OR MORE SERVINGS

This recipe comes from our colleague, talented cooking teacher Claudia Stromberg. The dressing prevents the peaches from darkening.

1½	cups raw converted rice
¾	cup raisins
8 to 10	peaches peeled and cut into bite-size pieces
1	pound cooked ham, cut into bite-size strips
1	cup thinly sliced celery
6	scallions, thinly sliced

DRESSING:

½	cup sour cream
½	cup mayonnaise
¼	cup mango chutney (including semi-liquid portion), chopped
1½	teaspoons curry powder

Cook rice in 3¾ cups water in a covered saucepan for about 22 minutes or until rice is just done and liquid is absorbed. Stir in raisins, transfer to a mixing bowl, and cool.

Combine the dressing ingredients and stir into the cooled rice along with the peaches, ham, celery, and scallions. Refrigerate overnight.

To Prepare in Advance: Refrigerate up to 24 hours.

 *Fresh Figs and Cherries*

These two summer fruits require no fuss to eat, so they lend themselves beautifully to enjoyment while sailing. They may be served with the salad, with the cheese and crackers as a snack, or any time the mood strikes.

Cheese Wedges and Crackers

Choose a variety of at least three cheeses, such as Cheddar, Swiss, and dill-flavored Havarti. Cut into 2-ounce portions and wrap airtight in plastic wrap. Pack at least two varieties of crackers, plain or lightly seasoned, with cheeses in a noncrushable container and keep in a cool place. Serve at room temperature for best flavor.

Rocky Road Clusters

FOR 12 CANDIES

Natalie Haughton, Food Editor of the Los Angeles Daily News, brought us a holiday basket of goodies containing these crunchy tidbits with a hint of peanut butter.

> 2 cups (12 ounces) semisweet chocolate pieces
> ½ cup crunchy peanut butter
> 12 regular marshmallows

Butter 12 muffin cups or line them with frilled paper liners.

Use scissors or a knife dipped in cold water to cut the marshmallows into quarters. In top of a double boiler, combine chocolate pieces and peanut butter. Heat over hot but not boiling water until melted, stirring occasionally. Remove pan from water. Stir in marshmallows to distribute evenly. Immediately spoon chocolate mixture into muffin cups. Refrigerate.

To Prepare in Advance: Store in a cool place in an airtight container for up to 3 days, in refrigerator for up to 3 weeks, or freeze for up to 3 months.

A U T U M N

AT the very end of summer, when light frosts make the leaves turn color, we find Indian corn to hang on the front door and begin to anticipate long walks, the sound of crunching leaves underfoot, and the arrival in the markets of brightly colored produce which too has felt the frost. Pumpkins remind us that Halloween is fast approaching; the new crop of walnuts will appear in plum puddings and fruitcakes to be aged and sprinkled with Cognac or rum during the months before Christmas. Nuts are set out in a bowl near the fireplace with a nutcracker for impromptu nibbling.

In the garden, it is time to harvest the last of our summer's crop of herbs for drying in bunches hanging from our kitchen rafters among the old copper pots. We cut chrysanthemums to decorate the dining table, and also to garnish platters of Paul's wonderful stir-fry dishes which are so appealing in the newly crisp weather. We stop at roadside stands for the last of the summer's harvest to make preserves—chutneys, jams, and apple butter—to be served throughout the fall and winter and to give as gifts.

We plan ahead to Thanksgiving, our favorite holiday. In fact, we send out Thanksgiving cards instead of Christmas cards, with a picture of the three of us enjoying the preparation of a typical feast. That menu is almost always the same—everyone insists on turkey with pecan stuffing accompanied by giblet gravy, peas, apple and yam casserole, raw cranberry relish. But we are more adventurous in planning our other outings and entertainments. The last outdoor barbecue of the year might be given in a friend's yard, where we can all enjoy the colors of the season. Our newfound passion for pizza inspires an idea for a gathering of friends in the playroom. A fishing expedition for the two of us sounds like a wonderful outdoorsy idea. And a larger party with a Southwestern theme and lots of robust food will make entertaining easy. The end of summer marks the beginning of big fall appetites.

A COUNTRY WESTERN BARBECUE
(FOR 10 TO 12)

Wine and Beer

*Raw Vegetables in Cherry Tomato Baskets
with Yogurt Vegetable Dip*

Barbecued Beef Ribs

Hacienda Brown Rice with Sour Cream, Cheese, and Chiles

Red, Green, and Orange Cabbage Slaw

Fiesta Corn Salad

Applesauce Spice Cake with Fresh Apple Topping

A COUNTRY WESTERN BARBECUE

For this down-home celebration you won't spend all afternoon polishing your crystal, nor are you expected to put a mirror shine on your leather. More likely you'll be arranging some country-fresh daisies in a tin bucket, brown bottles of beer in a galvanized tub, and selecting some Western music for a full evening.

This menu is designed for an early fall day or early evening, and for what may be the last cook-out of the year. The setting can be a real ranch, a local park, or someone's backyard—wherever it's possible to enjoy the autumn leaves just beginning to turn. The point is to get outdoors and barbecue.

We're compulsive savers. We can't bear to throw away a new shoebox, or those green plastic containers that strawberries come in. Our favorite containers to hoard are the old-fashioned wooden cherry tomato baskets. They've got just the right feel when you fill them with raw vegetables and wedge a small container of dip into a corner. We give one to each guest, so they can wander a bit and not feel like they are standing in line for the appetizer.

The marinade for the barbecued beef ribs is non-cloying and robust, and really tastes homemade. These ribs alone could make your reputation. A large, shallow dish made of Mexican pottery holds a marvelous mixture of brown rice layered with sour cream, cheese, and chiles, always a delicious combination. Two ranch-style salads, a colorful slaw and a mixture of corn, onions, bell peppers, and chili powder, involve no last-minute preparation at all.

Dessert, a moist and spicy apple cake topped with cream cheese icing and studded with slices of red apple, is inspired by the crops of apples appearing in the markets. Chopped walnuts from the new harvest are pressed into the side. The cake looks like it won a prize at a state fair.

After dinner, a walk in the moonlight feels like the next best thing to saddling up the horses.

SHOPPING LIST

1 medium-size white onion
2 bunches scallions
2 bunches chives
9 carrots
  Assorted vegetables to serve
    with dip (1 jícama, 4 celery
    stalks or 2 medium fennel
    bulbs, 1 medium head
    broccoli, 6 to 8 mushrooms,
    2 zucchini or other summer
    squash, 2 baskets cherry
    tomatoes)
1 hothouse cucumber
16 wooden cherry tomato baskets
    (ask the produce manager
    for these)
  Fresh coriander (cilantro; about
    ⅓ cup chopped)
  Fresh parsley
3 pounds fresh ears of corn
½ head red cabbage
½ head green cabbage
6 medium tomatoes
3 medium-size green bell peppers
1 medium-size red bell pepper
3 fresh mild green chiles
    (California, Anaheim, or
    poblano)
1 red apple
24 to 36 meaty beef rib bones

1½ pounds Monterey Jack cheese
6 ounces sharp Cheddar cheese
4 ounces cream cheese
2 large eggs
4 sticks plus 1 tablespoon un-
    salted butter
3½ cups (28 ounces) sour cream
1 quart plain yogurt
3 packages (10 ounces each)
    frozen corn kernels (if not
    using fresh)
2 cups brown rice
1 box (1 pound) powdered sugar
1 cup (8 ounces) soy sauce
    (reduced-sodium type, if
    desired)
1 can (4 ounces) diced green
    chiles (if not using fresh)
1 cup raisins
2 cups chopped walnuts or
    pecans
2½ cups applesauce
  Fruit Fresh or granulated
    vitamin C
8 ounces mayonnaise
½ cup sweet pickle relish
  Wine
  Beer
  Soft drinks

Staples

Brandy (2 to 3 teaspoons)
Olive oil (¼ cup)
Garlic (4 cloves)
Raspberry vinegar or red wine
   vinegar (¼ cup)
Red wine vinegar (¼ cup)
Vanilla (1 teaspoon)
Light corn syrup (2
   tablespoons)
All-purpose flour (3 cups)
Sugar (1 cup plus 2 teaspoons)
Dark brown sugar (1 cup firm-
   ly packed)
Baking soda (1 tablespoon)

Cinnamon (1 tablespoon)
Whole nutmeg (1 teaspoon
   freshly grated)
Ground cloves (1 teaspoon)
Onion powder (2 tablespoons)
Chili powder (2 teaspoons)
Ground cumin (2½ teaspoons)
Salt
Black pepper

DO-AHEAD TIMETABLE

Up to a week ahead: Bake apple cake

Up to five days ahead: Make dip. Prepare slaw

Three days ahead: Make rice casserole. Make corn salad

Two days ahead: Marinate ribs

One day ahead: Cut vegetables for dip

Day of the party: Arrange vegetables in cherry tomato baskets. Frost cake
   and top with apples

Just before leaving for the barbecue: Pack ice chests

Just before guests arrive: Ice wine, beer, and soft drinks

During the party: Barbecue ribs

 *Raw Vegetables in Cherry Tomato Baskets with Yogurt Vegetable Dip*

FOR 10 TO 12 SERVINGS

We enjoy finding new ways to give each guest an individual container of vegetables and dip, avoiding crowding and dripping. For this menu we recommend wooden cherry tomato baskets.

YOGURT VEGETABLE DIP (makes 6 cups):

1   hothouse cucumber, seeded
2   teaspoons salt
1   quart plain yogurt
2   teaspoons ground cumin
1   teaspoon butter
1   medium-size green bell pepper, seeds and membranes
        removed, diced
2   firm-ripe tomatoes, diced
1   bunch chives, snipped
2   tablespoons minced fresh parsley
1   tablespoon minced fresh coriander (cilantro)
2   teaspoons sugar
    Salt and freshly ground black pepper to taste

RAW VEGETABLES (use an assortment of the following, keeping in
        mind a variety of colors and textures):

4   carrots, cut into spears or curls
1   medium jícama, peeled and cut into ½-inch spears
4   celery stalks *or* 2 medium fennel bulbs, if available, cut
        into spears
1   medium head broccoli, cut into florets
6 to 8   mushrooms, quartered lengthwise
2   medium-size summer squash (zucchini, crookneck, or
        pattypan), cut into thin, diagonal slices
2   baskets cherry tomatoes with stems

112

To make the dip, chop or grate the cucumber. Toss with 2 teaspoons salt and let stand at room temperature for 10 to 15 minutes to draw out excess moisture. Place in rinsed cheesecloth or a clean kitchen towel and squeeze out as much of its liquid as possible. Stir gently into the yogurt (over-stirring thins yogurt). In a small skillet gently cook the cumin in the butter for 1 to 2 minutes to remove the raw flavor of the spice. Add it to the yogurt along with the other ingredients. Refrigerate for an hour or more for the flavors to develop.

Arrange vegetables in cherry tomato baskets, nestling in one corner a small container, such as a votive light holder (red looks great—see photograph), which can be used to hold the dip.

To Prepare in Advance: Arrange vegetables in cherry tomato baskets, cover with damp paper towels, and place each in a separate plastic bag. Refrigerate up to 24 hours. The dip will keep up to 5 days in the refrigerator.

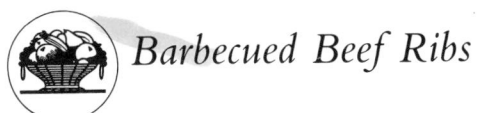

Barbecued Beef Ribs

FOR 10 TO 12 SERVINGS

Beef rib bones are meaty and delicious, and take only minutes to cook. Our good friend, novelist Genvieve Davis, shared her marinade with us.

24 to 36 meaty beef rib bones (2 to 3 per person)

VIVI'S MARINADE:

1 cup soy sauce (see Note)
½ cup (1 stick) unsalted butter, melted
3 garlic cloves, minced or pressed
2 tablespoons onion powder
½ teaspoon freshly ground black pepper

Note: We use Kikkoman reduced-sodium soy sauce (green label), available at most supermarkets. Because it contains less salt—about half that of regular soy—it should be refrigerated for storage.

Use one or more large, heavy plastic bags to marinate the ribs in—wastebasket liners do nicely. Set the bag(s) in a roasting pan in case a bag springs a leak. Place the ribs in the bag(s), combine the marinade ingredients, and pour over the ribs. Allow to marinate at least 3 hours at room temperature (or overnight in the refrigerator), turning the bag(s) two or three times.

Barbecue over greyed coals for about 5 to 10 minutes on each side, or until meat is medium-rare when tested.

Variation: If you prefer pork ribs, buy 12 to 16 ounces of meaty ribs per person. Brush with marinade and bake at 300°F for 45 minutes. Remove from the pan of drippings. (This may be done a day or two ahead of time and the ribs cooled and refrigerated, ready to take to the site.) To finish cooking, brush with more marinade and broil or grill 15 minutes longer, turning ribs often.

To Prepare in Advance: The ribs may marinate up to 2 days in the refrigerator.

Hacienda Brown Rice with Sour Cream, Cheese, and Chiles

FOR 12 SERVINGS

Butter for baking dish
3 fresh mild green chiles (California, Anaheim, or poblano) *or* 1 can (4 ounces) diced green chiles
2 cups raw brown rice, cooked (6 cups cooked)
3 cups sour cream
   Salt and freshly ground black pepper
1 pound Monterey Jack cheese, shredded
1 bunch scallions (including some of the green tops), sliced
6 ounces sharp Cheddar cheese, shredded

Preheat oven to 350°F.

If using fresh chiles, they must be roasted and peeled. *All chiles should be handled with care* because they contain a chemical irritant that can cause discomfort or even a painful rash in those who are highly sensitive. Wear rubber gloves in handling them until you determine your degree of sensitivity. To remove the peel from chiles, char the skin over a direct flame, on a rack over an electric burner, or under the broiler, turning often to blacken the skin evenly. Place the chiles in a plastic bag and let them steam for a few minutes, separating the flesh from the skin. Peel by scraping off the skin with the back of a knife on a flat surface or by rubbing under cold running water. Most of the hotness is in the membranes and seeds, so slit the chiles down one side and open to remove them if you want a milder flavor. Dice the chiles finely.

Spread 2 cups of the cooked rice evenly over the bottom of a buttered 4-quart baking dish (a dish measuring 13x9 inches will do nicely). Spread 1 cup of the sour cream over the rice and sprinkle generously with salt and pepper. Cover with half the chiles, Jack cheese, and scallions, evenly distributed. Repeat the layers in the same order, beginning with the rice. Top with the last third of the rice, followed by the last cup of sour cream. Season with salt and pepper and top the casserole with the shredded Cheddar.

Bake for about 20 minutes, or until the cheese is melted and the rice is heated all the way through.

To Prepare in Advance: Store the casserole, baked or unbaked, in the refrigerator for up to 3 days. Rewarm by baking, covered, at the same temperature for the same length of time as in the recipe. Take care not to overheat it when rewarming, or the sour cream may separate.

 ## Red, Green, and Orange Cabbage Slaw

FOR 10 TO 12 SERVINGS

½ head red cabbage, quartered and cored
½ head green cabbage, quartered and cored
1 bunch scallions, very thinly sliced
2 carrots, peeled and finely grated
½ cup chopped fresh parsley

DRESSING:

1 cup mayonnaise
½ cup sour cream (yogurt can be substituted)

115

½ cup sweet pickle relish
¼ cup raspberry vinegar *or* red wine vinegar
1 garlic clove, minced or pressed

Slice the cabbage quarters very, very thinly by hand or with the fine slicing blade of a food processor. Combine in a large mixing bowl with the other slaw ingredients.

Combine the dressing ingredients and pour over the slaw, tossing to coat thoroughly. Chill for at least 2 hours, tossing once or twice.

To Prepare in Advance: This tastes best if chilled 24 hours before serving. Store in the refrigerator up to 5 days.

Fiesta Corn Salad

FOR 10 TO 12 SERVINGS

3 pounds fresh ears of corn *or* 3 packages (10 ounces) frozen corn kernels
4 medium tomatoes, seeded and diced (do not peel)
1 medium-size white onion *or* 1 bunch scallions, minced
2 medium-size green bell peppers, seeded and finely diced
1 medium-size red bell pepper, seeded and finely diced *or* 1 jar (2 ounces) pimiento pieces, drained
¼ cup olive oil
¼ cup red wine vinegar
2 teaspoons chili powder
½ teaspoon ground cumin
8 ounces Monterey Jack cheese (plain or with jalapeños), cut into ½-inch dice
¼ cup chopped fresh coriander, (cilantro) or, if unavailable, fresh parsley

If using fresh corn, remove the outer husk and the silk. Cut lengthwise from the cob with a sharp knife. Drop into a large pot of boiling unsalted water and simmer for 3 minutes. Drain and cool. If using frozen corn, cook only until thawed; drain and cool. Place corn in mixing bowl with tomatoes, onion, and bell peppers. Combine olive oil, wine vinegar, chili powder, and cumin, whisking to blend, and pour over the vegetables. Toss until ingredients are coated, then fold in the cheese and cilantro or parsley.

For best flavor, serve at room temperature.

To Prepare in Advance: Salad can be refrigerated up to 3 days. Bring to room temperature before serving.

Applesauce Spice Cake with Fresh Apple Topping

FOR 12 OR MORE SERVINGS

Our daughter, Lexi, won a ribbon at the Hidden Hills Fiesta Bake Contest with this spicy marvel. The fresh apple slices that decorate the top are dipped into a mixture of ascorbic acid (vitamin C) and water to prevent darkening.

          1   cup (2 sticks) unsalted butter
          1   cup firmly packed dark brown sugar
          1   cup granulated sugar
          2   eggs
          3   cups all-purpose flour
          1   tablespoon baking soda
        ½   teaspoon salt
          1   tablespoon cinnamon
       1½   teaspoons freshly grated nutmeg
          1   teaspoon ground cloves
       2½   cups applesauce
          2   tablespoons light corn syrup
          1   cup raisins
          1   cup chopped walnuts

          CREAM CHEESE ICING:

          4   ounces cream cheese
          1   box (1 pound) powdered sugar (see Note 1)

½ cup (1 stick) unsalted butter
1 teaspoon vanilla
2 to 3 teaspoons brandy

DECORATION:

1 cup chopped walnuts
½ cup water
½ teaspoon granulated ascorbic acid (vitamin C) *or* Fruit Fresh
    (see Note 2)
1 red apple

Note 1: For best results, open a fresh box of powdered sugar to avoid sifting. It will be lump-free and much easier to beat into a smooth icing.
Note 2: This product, which keeps fruit from darkening, is sold in most supermarkets next to the canning supplies. It consists of ascorbic acid (vitamin C) with sugar added.

Preheat the oven to 325°F. Grease a loose-bottom 10-inch tube pan (angel food pan); line the bottom with waxed paper and grease the paper.

Combine the butter and sugars in the large bowl of an electric mixer and beat until very light and fluffy, stopping the motor from time to time to scrape down the sides of the bowl with a rubber spatula. Add the eggs one at a time, beating well after each addition. Sift together the flour, soda, salt, and spices. Mix together the applesauce and corn syrup and add to the butter mixture alternately with the dry ingredients, beating constantly. Fold in the raisins and nuts.

Pour the batter into the prepared pan. Bake for 70 to 75 minutes, or until a pick inserted in the center of the cake comes out clean. Cool completely in the pan. Turn out onto serving plate and peel off paper. This cake tastes best if kept for at least 24 hours at room temperature, wrapped in plastic.

To make the icing, place all the icing ingredients in a bowl and beat until smooth. Spread icing over the cooled cake and decorate the sides with the chopped nuts.

To decorate with apple slices, combine ½ cup water with ½ teaspoon granulated ascorbic acid (crush 2 to 3 vitamin C tablets if that is what you have on hand) or with ½ teaspoon Fruit Fresh. Core the apple, but do not peel. Using

a thin, sharp knife, cut the apple into very thin wedges and drop them into the ascorbic acid mixture. Blot dry and carefully arrange the apple slices on the top of the cake (see photograph).

To Prepare in Advance: This cake is very moist and improves with age if refrigerated for up to a week, without icing and apple topping. It may also be frozen for up to 3 months; (if iced, wrap cake after it is solidly frozen). The apple slices for decoration should be added no more than 12 hours before serving so they stay fresh looking.

A PIZZA PARTY FOR FAMILY AND FRIENDS
(FOR 8 TO 10)

Soft Drinks and Beer

Antipasto Platter with "Scallioned" Salami

Pizza Quattro Stagione
(Four Seasons Pizza)

Vegetarian Pizza with Wholewheat Crust

Super Salad Bowl with Creamy Garlic Dressing

---

*Ice Cream Sundae Spectacular
with Claudia's Hot Fudge, Raspberry Sauce,
and Fresh Pineapple Sauce*

A Pizza Party for Family and Friends

At least once every autumn our daughter, Lexi, will invite her two best friends, their dates, and all their parents over to our house for an evening of homemade pizza and old-time games.

The pizza is the easy half of the agenda. When the gang arrives, Lexi explains the fundamental rules of flattening the dough with fingertips and spinning it up in the air (only for those with a sense of daring). We then hold our own "Pizza Olympics": Guests create their masterpieces while nibbling on a spectacular antipasto platter, which is assembled around a candle nestled in a red bell pepper.

Two pizza recipes are included here. One is divided into four sections, representing the four seasons, and topped with ingredients to represent them. The other, a vegetarian pizza made with a wholewheat crust, is colorful, very fresh tasting, and always a big hit. Salad with a creamy garlic dressing and croutons complements the main course.

Dessert is a favorite of young and old alike: ice cream sundaes with a choice of sauces and toppings.

The other half of our planned activities is a charades contest, the adults against the teenagers. Kids are so smart these days, we usually don't have a chance!

SHOPPING LIST

2   heads Boston or Bibb lettuce
1   head red-leaf or salad bowl
       lettuce
1   head romaine lettuce
3   red bell peppers (one large
       pepper should stand upright
       to hold candle)
4   bunches large scallions
2   or 3 radishes
1   small brown onion
1   small red onion
2   to 3 celery stalks
    Fresh parsley
    Fresh basil (1 tablespoon
       minced)
    Fresh oregano (2 teaspoons
       minced)
12 ounces mushrooms
1   medium eggplant
4   to 6 tiny carrots
1   basket cherry tomatoes
1   small head cauliflower and/or
    1 small head broccoli
2   lemons (for juice)
    Vegetables for salad, as desired
    Assorted fresh fruits for
       sundaes (48 small cut pieces)
4   baskets raspberries
½   ripe pineapple
8   ounces Italian sausage (sweet
       or hot)
6   ounces thinly sliced Italian dry
       salami
6   ounces thinly sliced pepperoni
       or other dry sausage
8   ounces cream cheese
12 ounces shredded low moisture–
       part skim mozzarella cheese

    Parmesan cheese (for 6 table-
       spoons grated)
2   cups (16 ounces) heavy cream
2   sticks butter
    Assorted ice cream flavors (to
       make 24 scoops)
2   packages (10 ounces each)
       frozen raspberries (if not
       using fresh)
1   package (9 ounces) frozen
       artichoke hearts
3   to 4 ounces frozen or
       preserved pesto or
       ingredients to make fresh
       pesto (see Note 2, page 129)
8   ounces light corn syrup
8   to 10 slices of bread for
       croutons (optional)
1   cup Dutch process cocoa
2   packages active dry yeast
12 ounces bittersweet chocolate
    Garnishes for sundaes, as
       desired
1   can (6 ounces) tomato paste
1   can (8 ounces) tomato sauce
16 ounces mayonnaise
1   cup Mediterranean-style olives
       or pitted black olives
2   cups bottled red cherry peppers
       (or 1 basket cherry
       tomatoes)
4   ounces sun-dried tomatoes
       (optional)
½   cup dry vermouth or white
       wine
    Beer
    Soft drinks

Staples

Garlic (4 cloves)

Olive oil (6 tablespoons, plus
    ½ cup if making croutons)

Red wine vinegar (2
    tablespoons)

Dijon mustard (1 tablespoon)

Clover honey or molasses
(1 tablespoon), optional

Sesame or sunflower seed
(2 teaspoons)

Light brown sugar (1 cup
    firmly packed)

Granulated sugar
(2½ tablespoons)

Superfine sugar (if needed to
    sweeten pineapple)

3 cups bread flour or all-
    purpose flour

1 cup wholewheat flour

Cornmeal (1 to 2 tablespoons)

Arrowroot (2 teaspoons) or
    cornstarch (1 tablespoon)

Dried basil (1 teaspoon, if fresh
    not available)

Dried oregano (½ teaspoon, if
    fresh not available)

Salt

Cracked black pepper (2
    teaspoons)

Vanilla (4 teaspoons)

From a variety store

1 votive candle and holder

DO-AHEAD TIMETABLE

Up to a month ahead: Make and freeze pizza dough. Make fudge sauce

Up to a week ahead: Make salad dressing

Up to four days ahead: Make scallion filling

Three days ahead: Make raspberry sauce. Make fresh pineapple sauce

One day ahead: Arrange ice cream balls on serving platter. Arrange salami
    with scallion filling on platter. Chill beer and soft drinks. Thaw
    pizza dough

Day of the party: Assemble salad in bowl (3 to 4 hours). Cut red pepper for
    candle

Just before the party: Bring salami platter to room temperature. Assemble
    pizzas (2 hours) before and refrigerate

During the party: Bake pizzas. Toss salad

 *Antipasto Platter with "Scallioned" Salami*

MAKES ABOUT 30 INDIVIDUAL APPETIZERS

This colorful platter is designed around a red bell pepper-enclosed candle. Spectacular-looking "lilies" are edible.

SALAMI WITH SCALLION FILLING:

4   large scallions, including some of the green tops
8   ounces cream cheese
6   ounces thinly sliced Italian dry salami (measuring about 2½ inches in diameter)

TO GARNISH AND SERVE:

1   large, perfect red bell pepper, to hold a candle (choose one that will stand upright)
1   cup Mediterranean-style olives *or* pitted black olives
2   cups bottled red cherry peppers, drained, *or* 1 basket cherry tomatoes

SALAMI SCALLION LILIES:

12 large scallions

For the salami with filling, clean the scallions and cut into 1-inch lengths. Place in a food processor fitted with the steel blade and chop finely. (Lacking a food processor, chop the scallions by hand very finely.) Add the cream cheese and blend thoroughly.

Place about a teaspoonful of the scallion-cheese mixture on a slice of salami. Fold in half like a taco. Use about half the filling for 18 slices of salami, reserving remaining filling and salami for Salami Scallion Lilies.

To make a red bell pepper candle, use a sharp paring knife to cut out and discard the stem of the pepper, leaving an opening large enough to insert a votive candle and holder. Place the candle in the hollow.

Arrange the cheese-filled salami around the red pepper candle on a platter. Border the pepper with a row of olives and red cherry peppers or cherry tomatoes.

To make salami-scallion lilies, clean the scallions, trimming away the root tip but leaving the long green shoots. Spread the remaining salami slices on one side with the remaining cream cheese mixture. Fold one salami slice, cheese side in, around the white part of each scallion (see photograph). Chill the "lilies," seam down, until the cheese is firm enough to hold the salami in place.

Arrange "lilies" on antipasto platter. Light the candle just before guests arrive.

To Prepare In Advance: The entire platter may be prepared the night before your party. Cover with a damp towel and place in a large plastic bag (such as a wastebasket bag). Refrigerate until 30 to 45 minutes before serving.

 # Creating a Pizza Oven at Home

In the following recipes we have given instructions for baking pizza on large baking sheets or pizza pans that have been sprinkled with cornmeal to absorb excess liquid from the crust.

You can create an authentic pizza oven by placing a pizza stone (available at department stores and gourmet cookware shops) or a 14-inch square *unglazed* Mexican tile, about ¾ inch thick, in the bottom third of the oven. The tile absorbs moisture from the dough, creating a crisp crust. The oven and tile should be preheated to 450°F for about an hour before baking the pizza. For this method you will need a wooden paddle, called a "peel," for transferring the dough on and off the tile. If sprinkled with a little cornmeal, the pizza will slide right off when you tap the handle.

 ## *Pizza* Quattro Stagione *(Four Seasons Pizza)*

MAKES ONE 12-INCH PIZZA; 8 SLICES

This is a very popular style of pizza in Italy. The four seasons refer to the four different toppings, arranged in sections. We've experimented with many pizza doughs, and this quick and simple one is our favorite.

BASIC PIZZA CRUST:

2	cups bread flour or unbleached all-purpose flour
2	teaspoons sugar
½	teaspoon salt
1½	teaspoons active dry yeast
⅔	cup warm water (105°F to 115°F)
1	tablespoon olive oil
	Cornmeal for the pan

QUICK PIZZA SAUCE:

2	tablespoons olive oil
1	small onion, minced
2	garlic cloves, minced or pressed
1	can (6 ounces) tomato paste
1	can (8 ounces) tomato sauce
½	cup dry vermouth or white wine
2	tablespoons minced fresh parsley
1	tablespoon minced fresh basil *or* ½ teaspoon dried basil, crumbled
2	teaspoons minced fresh oregano *or* ½ teaspoon dried oregano, crumbled
½	teaspoon sugar

TOPPINGS:

1	cup (4 ounces) shredded low moisture–part skim mozzarella cheese

1 package (9 ounces) frozen artichoke hearts, thawed and
  blotted dry but not cooked
6 ounces pepperoni or other dry sausage, thinly sliced into
  rounds
6 ounces mushrooms, sliced
8 ounces Italian sausage (sweet or hot), cooked and cut
  diagonally into ½-inch slices
2 to 3 tablespoons olive oil
2 tablespoons freshly grated Parmesan cheese

For crust, combine the flour, sugar, and salt in a mixing bowl or in the bowl of a food processor and blend briefly. Sprinkle yeast into warm water, then stir until dissolved. Add olive oil to the yeast mixture. If mixing by hand, add the liquid gradually to the flour mixture while stirring with a wooden spoon, then turn the dough out onto a lightly floured surface and knead until smooth and satiny, about 3 to 4 minutes. If using a food processor, turn machine on and pour the liquid through the feed tube, processing until the dough forms a ball and cleans the side of the machine. Knead it in the machine for 30 seconds or so, then turn dough out onto a lightly floured surface. Cover with a mixing bowl or plastic wrap, leaving room to rise, and let rest for 15 to 30 minutes.

Meanwhile, place rack in bottom third of oven and preheat to 425°F for 30 minutes.

For sauce, heat the olive oil in a medium skillet and sauté the onion until transparent. Add the garlic and sauté briefly, then add all remaining ingredients. Simmer for about 20 minutes, or until thickened. Cool.

Lightly sprinkle a heavy pizza pan, baking sheet, or wooden "peel" (paddle used to slide pizza onto hot oven tile) with cornmeal. Punch down dough. On a lightly floured surface, press the dough into a flat disc, then use fingertips, pressed into the surface of the dough, to stretch gradually to a diameter of 12 inches. Turn the disc of dough over frequently while continuing to press the entire surface. Place on top of cornmeal on the baking pan or peel.

Spoon the cooled pizza sauce over the dough. Cover with shredded mozzarella. Divide the pizza into quarters by marking gently with the back of a knife through the sauce. Arrange each topping separately in one quarter, creating neat triangles of the four fillings—artichoke hearts, pepperoni, mushrooms, and Italian sausage—leaving a 1-inch margin all around. Lightly brush olive oil over all the toppings. Sprinkle evenly with Parmesan.

Bake for 15 to 25 minutes, until the crust is browned and crisp. Let stand for a few minutes before slicing.

To Prepare In Advance: Make the dough the morning of your party, let it rise once, then punch it down and keep it in the refrigerator in 8-ounce balls. About 2 hours before the party bring dough to room temperature. The pizza may be assembled on its baking pan up to 30 minutes before baking. Cover with a towel and leave at room temperature (this will create a thicker crust). Pizza may be baked several hours ahead and reheated for serving, but flavor and texture are at their best when pizza is freshly baked.

 *Vegetarian Pizza with Wholewheat Crust*

MAKES ONE 12-INCH PIZZA; 8 SLICES

This is one of the most attractive and delicious pizzas we've ever created.

WHOLEWHEAT CRUST:

1 cup bread flour or unbleached all-purpose flour
1 cup wholewheat flour
1 tablespoon honey or molasses *or* 2 teaspoons sugar (see Note 1)
1 teaspoon salt
1½ teaspoons active dry yeast
⅔ cup warm water (105 to 115°F)
1 tablespoon olive oil

TOPPING (use any or all):

¼ to ⅓ cup pesto (see Note 2)
1 medium eggplant, halved lengthwise and cut into ½-inch-thick slices (salt and weight for 30 minutes, then rinse, brush with olive oil, and bake in a single layer at 400°F for 20 to 30 minutes, or until browned)

¼ cup freshly grated Parmesan cheese

2 to 3 medium mushrooms, sliced lengthwise

2 medium-size red bell peppers, roasted and peeled (see Note to Torta d'Alba recipe, page 15)

4 to 6 tiny carrots, halved lengthwise and steamed or microwaved until barely tender

1 to 2 cups cauliflower and/or broccoli florets, steamed or microwaved until barely tender

1½ cups (6 ounces) shredded low moisture–part skim mozzarella cheese

½ cup (2 ounces) shredded Cheddar cheese (or additional mozzarella)

A sprinkling of sesame or sunflower seed

Sun-dried tomatoes, including some of the oil from the jar (see Note 2 to Tabouli recipe), optional

Note 1: Substituting honey or molasses for sugar results in a softer crust, so we usually opt for sugar.

Note 2: Pesto is an uncooked garlic and herb sauce used in Italian cooking. It is available frozen or vacuum-packed in jars in Italian delis and some supermarkets. If fresh basil is available, make pesto quickly in the blender or food processor by combining 1 cup firmly packed fresh basil leaves, ¼ cup fresh parsley leaves, ¼ cup fine-quality olive oil, 2 tablespoons pine nuts or walnuts, 1 garlic clove, ½ teaspoon salt and ⅓ cup freshly grated Parmesan cheese, and processing to a paste consistency. Pesto may be refrigerated for up to a week or frozen for up to 3 months.

Make the dough in exactly the same manner as Basic Pizza Crust (with Pizza *Quattro Stagione* recipe, this menu), adding the honey or molasses with the liquid to the dry ingredients. Stretch the dough and place on pan or peel as directed.

Preheat oven to 425°F, with rack in bottom third of oven, for 30 minutes.

Spread the pesto over the dough and arrange the remaining toppings over the dough in the order listed. Bake for approximately 20 to 25 minutes, or until the crust is browned and crisp. Let stand a few minutes before slicing.

To Prepare In Advance: Make the dough, let it rise once, then punch it down and keep it in the refrigerator in 8-ounce balls. About 2 hours before the party bring dough to room temperature. The pizza may be assembled on its baking pan up to 30 minutes before baking. Cover with a towel and leave at room temperature (this will create a thicker crust). Pizza may be baked several hours ahead and reheated for serving, but flavor and texture are at their best when pizza is freshly baked.

Super Salad Bowl with Creamy Garlic Dressing

FOR 8 TO 10 SERVINGS

The pleasure of serving a large salad is that you can add such varied ingredients.

2	heads Boston or Bibb lettuce
1	head red-leaf or salad bowl lettuce
1	head romaine lettuce
4	ounces mushrooms, cut lengthwise into ¼-inch-thick slices
1	bunch scallions (including some of the green tops), thinly sliced
2 or 3	radishes, thinly sliced
1	basket cherry tomatoes, stemmed and halves
1	small red onion, thinly sliced
	Carrots, celery, etc., as desired
	Croutons (see Buffet Salad Bowl Caesar), optional

CREAMY GARLIC DRESSING (makes 3 cups):

2	cups mayonnaise
2	tablespoons red wine vinegar
2	tablespoons fresh lemon juice
1	tablespoon Dijon mustard
2	teaspoons sugar
2	teaspoons cracked black pepper
2	garlic cloves, minced or pressed, or more to taste
	Salt to taste

Rinse all the greens and drain them well. Cut or tear into bite-size pieces, wrap in paper towels and place in sealed plastic bags for refrigerator storage.

Several hours before serving, place the remaining salad ingredients in the bottom of your salad bowl and place the mixed greens on top. Cover the greens with damp paper towels and refrigerate until ready to serve.

Combine dressing ingredients, seasoning to taste with salt and additional garlic if desired.

Toss the greens and vegatables together just before placing on the buffet table. Serve the dressing on the side.

To Prepare In Advance: The greens will stay crisp and fresh up to 4 days in the refrigerator, if washed and sealed in storage bags as directed. Prepare the remaining vegetables the morning of the party; slice the mushrooms, but reassemble them in their original shape to keep them from drying out until tossed. The dressing will keep indefinitely in the refrigerator, but for best flavor bring to room temperature before serving.

Ice Cream Sundae Spectacular

FOR 8 TO 10 SERVINGS

Guests will love making their own sundaes from a large platter of ice creams and fruit.

> About 24 large scoops of ice cream in assorted flavors
> About 48 bite-size pieces of fresh fruit in season: include whole berries, sliced melon, sliced bananas (dipped in lemon juice to prevent discoloration), sliced kiwi
> Claudia's Hot Fudge (recipe follows)
> Raspberry Sauce (recipe follows)
> Fresh Pineapple Sauce (recipe follows)
> Roasted peanuts, coconut, and other garnishes, as desired.

Arrange the ice cream scoops in a shallow serving dish and keep frozen. Remove from the freezer 15 minutes before serving. Accompany with a platter of attractively arranged fruits, sauces, and any other desired toppings.

To Prepare In Advance: Store the scoops of ice cream on their serving platter in the freezer for up to 24 hours. The fruit platter, covered tightly with plastic wrap, may be refrigerated up to 4 hours. Bring to room temperature before serving.

Claudia's Hot Fudge

MAKES ABOUT 5 CUPS; UP TO 20 SERVINGS

Cooking instructor Claudia Stromberg gave us her recipe for this outrageously good ice cream topping.

    1   cup light corn syrup
    1   cup firmly packed light brown sugar
    2   cups heavy cream
    1   cup Dutch process cocoa (see Note 1)
    1   cup (2 sticks) butter
    12 ounces bittersweet chocolate (see Note 2), broken into pieces
    4   teaspoons vanilla

Note 1: Dutch process cocoa has been treated with alkali for a mellow flavor; the phrase "processed with alkali" appears on the label. Droste is the most widely available brand.

Note 2: Claudia uses Rykoff International bittersweet chocolate, sold in gourmet specialty shops. Other excellent brands include Tobler Tradition and Lindt Excellence, sold in 3-ounce bars in the candy section of many supermarkets.

Combine corn syrup, brown sugar, 1⅓ cups of the cream, and the cocoa in a heavy saucepan. Bring to a simmer over medium heat and cook, stirring, for 5 minutes or until the mixture is thick and glossy. Remove from heat and stir in the butter. Allow to cool for a minute or two, then stir in the chocolate pieces and vanilla. Blend in the remaining cream after chocolate melts.

To Prepare In Advance: Cover and refrigerate for up to 6 weeks, or freeze indefinitely. Reheat in a double boiler or heavy saucepan, stirring often, just until hot.

Raspberry Sauce

MAKES ABOUT 2½ CUPS UP TO 10 SERVINGS

A tart and delicious sauce to complement many desserts.

4 baskets raspberries *or* 2 packages (10 ounces each) frozen
    raspberries, thawed
¼ cup sugar
2 teaspoons arrowroot *or* 1 tablespoon cornstarch
¼ cup cold water
¼ cup fresh lemon juice

Puree the raspberries in a blender or food processor. Sieve to remove seeds and place in a heavy small saucepan. Stir together the sugar and arrowroot or cornstarch then add the water, mixing to a paste; stir into the raspberries. Cook and stir over low heat until the sauce thickens slightly. Add the lemon juice. Serve hot or cold.

To Prepare In Advance: The sauce may be made 2 to 3 days ahead and refrigerated. Reheat gently in a heavy small saucepan if serving hot.

Fresh Pineapple Sauce

MAKES ABOUT 2½ CUPS UP TO 10 SERVINGS

This has a wonderful fresh flavor. Good over plain fruit, too.

½ fresh pineapple, peeled, cored, and cut into cubes
    Superfine sugar, if necessary

Place the pineapple cubes in blender or food processor fitted with the steel blade and puree. Sweeten if desired. Chill thoroughly.

To Prepare In Advance: Refrigerate, covered, in a nonmetal container for up to 3 days.

COOKING THE CATCH
(FOR 4)

Curried Cauliflower Soup

Pan-Fried Trout Amandine

Wild Rice Salad with Tarragon, Orange, and Pecans

Lemon Macadamia Loaf Cake

COOKING THE CATCH

Many of us have friends and neighbors who return home from fishing trips with more fish than they can fry. If they offer to share them, accept unhesitatingly and invite them to celebrate with this menu.

Let your lucky friends entertain you with their tales of walking across dewy meadows at dawn, heading toward a secret fishing spot in the crystal waters of a mountain lake, and "the one that got away," while you serve up mugs of steaming Curried Cauliflower Soup. Even if you and yours are only armchair fishermen, you can still create the occasion at home (sans stories) with a visit to the local fishmonger for some rainbow trout. They are cooked as they often are at campsites, with a coating of cornmeal and a garnish of sliced almonds. The salad that accompanies the trout, a combination of wild rice, pecans, and orange rind, is wonderful for any autumn occasion. The simple dessert is a tangy loaf of Lemon Macadamia Cake.

Should you decide to take this menu to your secret lakeside location and try *your* luck, the salad and dessert will travel comfortably in a backpack. You could even take a thermos of soup for fortification along the way.

SHOPPING LIST

Fresh parsley
1 large head cauliflower
1 shallot or 1 bunch fresh chives
1 small onion
1 stalk celery
3 large lemons
1 small thick-skinned orange (for rind)
4 whole trout, about 12 ounces each
2 eggs
3 sticks butter
⅓ cup milk
½ cup yellow cornmeal
½ cup white or brown rice
½ cup wild rice
¾ cup finely chopped macadamia nuts
¾ cup sliced or slivered almonds
½ cup pecan halves

Staples

Garlic (2 cloves)
Worcestershire sauce
Olive oil (¾ cup)
Dijon mustard (1 tablespoon)
Chicken or turkey broth (4 cups plus 2 tablespoons)
Champagne vinegar, white wine vinegar, or fresh lemon juice (¼ cup)
All-purpose flour (1½ cups)
Sugar (about 1⅓ cups)
Baking powder (1 teaspoon)
Dried tarragon (½ teaspoon)
Curry powder (1½ teaspoons)
Ground mace (pinch)
Whole nutmeg
Salt
Black pepper

DO-AHEAD TIMETABLE

Up to a month ahead: Make and freeze lemon cake

Up to three days ahead: Prepare wild rice salad. Make soup

One day ahead: Thaw lemon cake

Just before serving: Heat soup. Pan-fry trout

Curried Cauliflower Soup

FOR 4 SERVINGS

We serve this fragrant and spicy mixture often, not only hot as a soup, but chilled as a dip for raw vegetables.

        1   tablespoon butter
    1½   teaspoons curry powder
        4   cups well-seasoned chicken or turkey broth (preferably
                    homemade—if canned, do not dilute)
        1   large head cauliflower, cored and cut into florets
        1   small onion, minced
        1   celery stalk, diced
            Worcestershire sauce to taste
            Freshly grated nutmeg to taste
            Salt to taste

Melt the butter in a heavy 3- to 4-quart saucepan and cook the curry powder briefly, stirring constantly, to bring out its full flavor. Add broth, cauliflower, onion, and celery. Cover and cook for 20 minutes, or until the cauliflower is very tender. Puree, in batches if necessary, in blender or food processor until very smooth. Return to saucepan and season to taste with Worcestershire, freshly grated nutmeg, and salt.

To Prepare in Advance: Refrigerate, covered, for up to 4 days. Reheat in a heavy saucepan, or serve chilled as a dip for vegetables.

 *Pan-Fried Trout Amandine*

FOR 4 SERVINGS

We like to use a combination of cornmeal and flour when pan-frying fish of any type. You will need an even-heating skillet, preferably nonstick. You may want to add a few capers or some fresh dill along with the almonds; both have a great affinity for trout.

4	whole trout, (about 12 ounces each) cleaned
½	cup yellow cornmeal
½	cup all-purpose flour
1	teaspoon salt
½	teaspoon freshly ground black pepper
¾	cup clarified butter (see Note)
¾	cup sliced or slivered almonds
1	lemon, halved

Note: Clarified butter does not spoil as does plain butter, and since it can stand a much higher temperature without burning it is better for frying. To obtain ¾ cup, melt 1 cup (2 sticks) butter in a saucepan over low heat, then let it rest for a minute or two off the heat. Skim off and discard any milk solids on top, then carefully pour the clear butter into a jar for storage, leaving the rest of the milk solids behind in the bottom of the pan.

Remove the heads from the trout if necessary for them to fit in the pan. Combine the cornmeal, flour, salt, and pepper on a plate or piepan. Dredge trout in the mixture and set aside for at least 10 minutes.

Melt about ⅓ of the clarified butter in a large skillet over medium heat. Add almonds and saute until light brown. Squeeze the juice of half a lemon over the almonds; turn out of the pan. Add half the remaining butter to the pan and pan-fry the trout, two at a time, for about 4 minutes on each side, or until the fish flakes easily and is well browned (trout should not be undercooked). Repeat with the remaining butter and trout. Transfer trout to a serving dishes. Pour the almond mixture over them and garnish with lemon wedges.

To Prepare in Advance: Clarify the butter and combine the seasoned flour mixture at your convenience.

 *Wild Rice Salad with Tarragon, Orange, and Pecans*

FOR 4 TO 6 SERVINGS

This salad just looks like autumn, and it goes well with most any menu. Wild rice is very expensive, so we stretch it by adding an equal portion of brown or white rice.

½ cup raw wild rice
½ cup raw brown or white rice
4 cups cold water
½ teaspoon salt
½ recipe (⅔ cup) Henri's Tarragon Dressing (see Spinach Salad with Raisins and Toasted Almonds)
½ cup toasted pecan halves
2 teaspoons grated or finely julienned orange rind
  Salt and freshly ground black pepper to taste

Rinse the wild rice thoroughly for several minutes in a strainer under cold running water. Place it in a medium saucepan with 4 cups cold water. Add ½ teaspoon salt, bring to a boil, then lower the heat and simmer, uncovered, for 15 minutes. If using brown rice, add it now and simmer, uncovered, for 45 minutes longer. If using white rice, allow wild rice to cook for 45 minutes, then add white rice and continue cooking for 15 minutes. Drain.

Pour the dressing over the warm rice, mixing it lightly but thoroughly. Fold in the pecans and orange rind. Season to taste with salt and pepper. Chill.

To serve, transfer to a serving dish. To create an attractive garnish for the edge of the dish, halve the grated orange lengthwise and remove white membrane. Cut into thin crosswise half rounds, positioning them around the rim of the bowl.

To Prepare in Advance: Refrigerate the salad, covered, up to 3 days. Garnish just before serving.

Lemon Macadamia Loaf Cake

MAKES ONE 8x4-INCH LOAF

This loaf cake stays moist and delicious for a long time.

       Shortening to grease pan
  1 cup sugar
  6 tablespoons (¾ stick) unsalted butter, melted
       Grated rind of 1 large lemon
  2 eggs
1½ cups sifted all-purpose flour
  1 teaspoon baking powder
  ¼ teaspoon salt
  ⅓ cup milk
  ¾ cup finely chopped macadamia nuts (see Note)

       GLAZE:

  ¼ cup fresh lemon juice
  ¼ cup sugar

Note: If nuts are salted, shake in a strainer, then rub in a clean towel.

Preheat the oven to 350°F. Grease an 8x4-inch loaf pan and line the bottom with waxed paper or foil; grease the paper or foil as well.

In a large mixing bowl, beat the sugar and melted butter for 1 minute. Beat in the eggs one at a time. Sift together the flour, baking powder, and salt and beat in alternately with the milk. Fold in the reserved lemon rind and chopped macadamias. Turn into the prepared pan.

Bake for 1 hour, or until the bread springs back when pressed in the center. Remove from the oven and cool for a few minutes. Meanwhile, combine the glaze ingredients; drizzle over the bread while still warm.

Cool the bread completely. Remove from pan and peel off waxed paper or foil. Wrap tightly in foil and refrigerate for 24 hours before slicing.

To Prepare in Advance: The loaf may be refrigerated, tightly wrapped in plastic and overwrapped with foil, for up to a month, or frozen for up to 6 months.

HALLOWEEN IN THE PLAYROOM
(FOR 16)
Children: Hot Apple Cider
Adults: Chilled Beer
Peanut Butter Popcorn

The Great Gourmet Burger
with Zucchini Relish★ and Assorted Toppings

Spinach Salad with Raisins and Toasted Almonds

Carrot Chocolate Chip Bundt Cake

★See Index

HALLOWEEN IN THE PLAYROOM

We have one child, our lovely daughter, Lexi. Just like parents everywhere, we've progressed through and been deeply involved with the yearly ritual of Halloween—the whole works, from fairy princess to ballerina to adorable green-nosed witch. How we have frozen, huddled in our parkas, as this flimsily-costumed, needle-legged sprite ran screeching with her friends through the neighborhood, door-to-door, demanding "trick or treat."

She has at last reached the age of reason. We are all nearing agreement that this Halloween a costume party at home is preferable to trick-or-treating, with, perhaps, the exception of a fast foray or two out into the darkness to refill coffers of candy. It's a habit that's hard to break.

We had a family conference to vote upon the menu; you can probably guess which one of us insisted upon hamburgers. We did, however, add some further touches in the way of unusual toppings and a wonderful leafy spinach salad with raisins and toasted almonds.

Dessert is a moist carrot cake studded with chocolate chips, and whatever goodies the kids have brought home.

SHOPPING LIST

24 leaves of lettuce
4 medium-size brown onions
3 medium-size and 1 small red onion
10 medium zucchini
4 medium tomatoes
2 medium-size green bell peppers
1 medium-size red bell pepper
1 medium jícama or 1 cup finely diced water chestnuts
2 pounds mushrooms
2 lemons (for juice)
2 pounds fresh spinach
Carrots (for 2 cups grated)
1 pound bacon
6 to 8 pounds ground beef chuck
1½ pounds sliced Swiss cheese
1½ pounds sliced sharp Cheddar cheese
3 to 4 ounces (or more) Roquefort cheese
1 stick butter
4 eggs
3 to 4 ounces semisweet chocolate chips
¼ cup chunky peanut butter
⅔ cup unpopped popcorn
1 can (8 ounces) crushed pine-apple in syrup
2 dozen hamburger buns or rolls
¼ cup Champagne vinegar or white wine vinegar (if not using lemon juice for salad dressing)
Assorted mustards (Dijon, Pommery, and Colman's, for example)

18 ounces cider vinegar
Olive oil (¾ cup)
16 ounces mayonnaise
1 jar (8 ounces) Dijon mustard (preferably Grey Poupon)
1 cup slivered almonds
½ cup chopped walnuts
½ cup roasted peanuts
1 cup raisins or dried currants
Apple cider
Beer

Staples

Garlic (2 cloves)
Vegetable oil (1¾ cups)
Dijon mustard (1 tablespoon)
Chicken broth (2 tablespoons)
Milk (1 tablespoon)
Powdered sugar (1 cup)
Salt (6 tablespoons)
Sugar (6 cups)
All-purpose flour (2¼ cups)
Cornstarch (1 tablespoon)
Baking powder (2 teaspoons)
Baking soda (1 teaspoon)
Dry mustard (1 tablespoon)
Celery salt (2 teaspoons)
Dried tarragon (½ teaspoon)
Cinnamon (2½ teaspoons)
Ground nutmeg (2 teaspoons)
Turmeric (2 teaspoons)
Ground mace (pinch)
Vanilla or almond extract (¼ teaspoon)

DO-AHEAD TIMETABLE

Up to a month ahead: Make Zucchini Relish. Bake and freeze cake

Up to three days ahead: Make popcorn. Toast almonds for salad

One day ahead: Form hamburger patties. Prepare salad dressing. Chill beer

Day of the party: Prepare toppings for hamburgers. Assemble salad in serving bowl

Just before the party: Heat apple cider

During the party: Cook hamburgers. Toss salad

 *Peanut Butter Popcorn*

MAKES ABOUT 16 CUPS (4 QUARTS)

This snack disappears in a hurry.

2 tablespoons (¼ stick) butter
¼ cup chunky peanut butter
⅔ cup unpopped popcorn, popped according to package directions
½ cup roasted peanuts
   Salt, if needed

Melt the butter in a small saucepan over low heat. Add the peanut butter, stirring for a minute or two until smooth, then drizzle the mixture over the popcorn. Toss lightly to mix. Add the peanuts and a light sprinkling of salt, if necessary, and toss again.

To Prepare in Advance: This is best freshly popped, but may be stored up to 3 days in an airtight container at room temperature.

The Great Gourmet Burger

MAKES 24 HAMBURGERS (ABOUT 16 SERVINGS)

Most people eat only one hamburger, but if there are teenagers present it's best to plan on two for them. Allow 1 pound of ground beef for 3 to 4 burgers.

6 to 8   pounds ground beef chuck
1   cup finely diced jícama or water chestnuts
1   medium-size green bell pepper, seeds and membranes removed, finely diced
24   hamburger rolls of your choice
  Zucchini Relish (see Index)

TOPPINGS (served buffet style):

24   leaves of lettuce
1½   pounds sliced Swiss cheese
1½   pounds sliced sharp Cheddar cheese
2   medium-size red onions, very thinly sliced
4   medium tomatoes, sliced
2   pounds mushrooms, thinly sliced lengthwise, and sautéed until tender in ¼ cup (½ stick) butter with 2 teaspoons fresh lemon juice, salt, and pepper
1   pound bacon, halved crosswise, cooked until crisp, and drained
  Roquefort mayonnaise (2 cups mayonnaise mixed with 3 to 4 ounces crumbled Roquefort cheese)
  Assorted mustards

In a large mixing bowl, combine ground meat with jícama or water chestnuts and green pepper. Divide into 24 portions and pat lightly into plump patties. Stack between squares of waxed paper, wrap airtight in plastic and refrigerate until cooking time.

Prepare the toppings and set out for guests to help themselves on a buffet table.

Grill or broil burgers about 4 inches from the heat for about 6 minutes on each side for medium, 5 minutes for rare, 7 minutes for well done. For cheeseburgers, add a slice of Swiss or Cheddar, or a sprinkling of Roquefort a minute or so before removing from grill.

To Prepare in Advance: Prepare the hamburger patties up to 24 hours in advance, wrap tightly, and refrigerate. The cheeses may be sliced and wrapped tightly for refrigerator storage, as may the Roquefort mayonnaise. Saute the mushrooms 3 to 4 hours ahead and reheat to serve.

 *Spinach Salad with Raisins and Toasted Almonds*

FOR 16 SERVINGS

Spinach holds up much better than other greens on a buffet table.

2 pounds fresh spinach, washed, dried, stemmed, and torn into pieces
1 small red onion, thinly sliced and separated into rings
1 cup raisins or dried currants, rinsed in hot water and drained
1 cup toasted slivered almonds
Henri's Tarragon Dressing (recipe follows)

Combine the salad ingredients in a salad bowl. Add enough dressing to just coat the spinach and toss well.

To Prepare in Advance: Place spinach in the salad bowl on top of the onions, raisins, and almonds. Cover with damp paper towels. Refrigerate for up to 24 hours before serving.

Henri's Tarragon Dressing

MAKES ABOUT 1⅓ CUPS

Our friend Henri Schley owns a restaurant in the South of France; we enjoy our evenings of cooking and dining together. Henri's dressing is excellent on many types of greens. If using it on salads that don't contain onions, add 1 minced shallot or 1 tablespoon snipped fresh chives to the dressing. His trick of warming dried herbs in a bit of chicken broth helps to bring out their maximum flavor.

2	tablespoons hot chicken broth
½	teaspoon dried tarragon, crumbled
	Pinch of ground mace
½	teaspoon sugar
2	garlic cloves, minced or pressed
1	tablespoon Dijon mustard
¼	cup Champagne vinegar, white wine vinegar, *or* fresh lemon juice
¾	cup olive oil

Pour the hot chicken stock over the tarragon, mace, and sugar in a small mixing bowl. Let stand for 5 minutes. Blend in the garlic, mustard, and vinegar. Add the oil gradually, whisking constantly, until the dressing is creamy and smooth.

To Prepare in Advance: Prepare up to 36 hours ahead and refrigerate. Bring to room temperature and shake before serving.

 *Carrot Chocolate Chip Cake*

MAKES ONE 10-INCH BUNDT OR TUBE CAKE

Since so many sweets appear on Halloween, one cake will probably suffice. You may wish to bake a second cake, just to be sure; you can always freeze any that is left.

	Butter and flour for pan
2	cups sifted all-purpose flour
2	cups sugar
2	teaspoons cinnamon
½	teaspoon freshly grated nutmeg
2	teaspoons baking powder
1	teaspoon baking soda
1	teaspoon salt
4	eggs
1½	cups vegetable oil
2	cups finely grated carrots
1	cup (one 8-ounce can) crushed pineapple, drained
½	cup chopped walnuts
½ to ¾	cup semisweet chocolate chips tossed with 2 teaspoons flour

GLAZE:

1	cup sifted powdered sugar (see Note)
1	tablespoon cold milk
¼	teaspoon vanilla or almond extract

Note: Powdered sugar is so light that it is difficult to sift through a flour sifter. It is easier to use a large-mesh strainer, shaking it or pressing it through with the back of a spoon.

Coat the inside of a 10-inch bundt or tube pan with butter and dust with flour. Preheat oven to 350°F.

In the large bowl of an electric mixer combine the flour, sugar, cinnamon, baking powder, baking soda, and salt. Beat in the eggs until thoroughly blended.

148

Add the oil ¼ cup at a time, beating constantly. Stir in the carrots and crushed pineapple. Fold in the walnuts. Turn the batter into the prepared pan.

Sprinkle the chocolate chips evenly over the surface of the cake (they will melt into the cake and lose their chip shape). Bake for 60 to 70 minutes, or until the top springs back when pressed. Cool 15 minutes in the pan, then turn cake out onto a rack to cool completely.

Combine the glaze ingredients, mixing until very smooth. Spoon the glaze over the cake, letting it drip decoratively down the sides.

To Prepare in Advance: Store the cake, covered, at room temperature for up to 2 days, or freeze. It is best to freeze the iced cake without a wrapping until the icing is hardened, then wrap securely for freezer storage.

A SOUTHWESTERN BUFFET
(FOR 16)

Iced Tea Garnished with Fresh Mint
Red and Chilled White Wine

Green Chile Dip
with Red, Yellow, Green, and Purple Dippers

Tortilla Chips

Southwestern Stroganoff
with Avocado, Cilantro, and Pomegranate

Beef Picadillo

Fiesta Rice Pilaf

Buffet Salad Bowl Caesar

Jicama, Cucumber, and Orange Salad

Lime Meringue Pie with Toasted Nut Crust

A SOUTHWESTERN BUFFET

The first ranchers had no land of their own, but grazed their horses and cattle on the free public range lands of the Southwest. The Homestead Act of 1862 changed all that by sending West wave upon wave of homesteaders who eventually fenced the land off. These homesteaders were English, Irish, French, Italian, German, you name it—they all came. They settled among people rich in Mexican/Spanish/Southwestern Indian traditions, from the Louisiana border up to Oregon, and they began to create a new cuisine. The Germans in Texas called theirs Tex-Mex. But it wasn't only the Texas Germans; it was every ethnic group. They all modified, added, compounded, and generally married their cooking to the foods that were native to the Southwest, and through generations of gastronomic selection have created the "New American Cuisine."

This old, slowly evolving Southwestern Cuisine has been quietly growing into adulthood, and it's just too good, too alive, not to be recognized. What's more, it's all-American. Imagine for a moment an Italian kitchen without tomatoes, the British Isles without potatoes, Africa without corn, India without chiles, Spain without sweet peppers, and France without beans—to list just a few of our Southwestern natives. None of these foods was known until the Americas were discovered, and they are the very heart of Southwestern cuisine.

Culinarily, America is coming of age.

We enjoy serving a buffet of foods that reflect the Southwestern culture, as this menu does. The dip is flavored with mild green chiles and is served warm with strips of bell pepper or with chips made from corn tortillas. The creamy Stroganoff, also spiked with chiles, is garnished with slices of avocado and pomegranate seeds. Another meat course is Picadillo, a traditional dish of seasoned ground meat with a surprising, almost sweet flavor from raisins, and there is a colorful pilaf. The buffet salad is an adaptation of the original Caesar salad, created in Tijuana on the California-Mexico border. A second salad, a mixture of jícama, cucumber, and orange, also has a Mexican origin.

Dessert is a lovely lime pie topped with a huge mound of meringue. It will remind one and all of the flavor of a Margarita, the festive Southwestern cocktail.

SHOPPING LIST

 3   carrots
 3   medium-size white onions
 3   large brown onions
 2   bunches scallions
 1   head garlic
 5   green bell peppers (one should
         be able to stand upright)
 3   each red and yellow bell
         peppers (one of each color
         should be able to stand
         upright)
 1   pound 10 ounces fresh mild
         green chiles (California,
         Anaheim or poblano)
 1½ pounds romaine lettuce
 ½   medium head red cabbage
 1   avocado
 1½ pounds jícama
 1   hothouse cucumber
     Fresh mint (to garnish iced tea)
     Fresh coriander (cilantro;
     ½ cup chopped), optional
     Fresh oregano (2 tablespoons
         chopped)
 3   oranges (preferably navel)
 6   to 8 limes (for 1 cup juice and
         1 teaspoon grated rind)
 2   large lemons (for juice)
 ½   pomegranate
 4   pounds lean ground beef
     Turkey breast or chicken (to
         make 4 cups cooked and
         shredded)

12   ounces Parmesan cheese
10   eggs
 2½ cups (20 ounces) sour cream
 3   sticks butter
 1   package (10 ounces) frozen
         peas
 3   cans (10¾ ounces each)
         condensed chicken broth (if
         not using homemade)
 4   cups white rice
 8   to 10 slices day-old bread
         (white, wholewheat, or
         French)
12   corn tortillas to make chips for
         dip (if not serving solely
         with bell pepper dippers)
 2   cans (15 ounces each) tomato
         sauce
 1   can (12 ounces) tomato paste
 4   cans (7 ounces each) whole
         green chiles (if not using
         fresh)
 1   can (2 ounces) flat anchovy
         fillets
 1   cup raisins
     Tea
 2⅓ cups olive oil
     Vegetable oil (for frying)
12   ounces mayonnaise
 ½   cup capers
 1½ cups slivered (not sliced)
         almonds
 6   ounces pecans, Brazil nuts, or
         walnuts

1½ cups dry Sherry
1 cup dry vermouth or 1½ cups
    dry white wine
White wine
Red wine

Staples

    Vinegar (1 teaspoon)
    Vanilla (½ teaspoon)
    All-purpose flour (½ cup)
    Sugar (1¾ cups)
    Cornstarch (½ cup)
    Cream of tartar (¼ teaspoon)
    Dried oregano (2 teaspoons, if
      fresh not available)

Chili powder (5 tablespoons)
Paprika
Celery salt (1 tablespoon)
Ground cumin (1 teaspoon)
Ground cloves (¼ teaspoon)
Cinnamon (¼ teaspoon)
Salt
Black pepper

DO-AHEAD TIMETABLE

Up to a month ahead: Freeze base for turkey Stroganoff. Freeze picadillo

Up to a week ahead: Make croutons for salad

Three days ahead: Make nut crust for pie

Two days ahead: Prepare green chile dip to point of baking. Make jícama, cucumber, and orange salad

One day ahead: Cut bell peppers for dipping. Make Caesar dressing. Prepare lettuce for salad

Day of the party: Cook rice in morning. Fill pie and top with meringue (8 hours ahead). Make iced tea. Chill white wine. Prepare pomegranate and cilantro to garnish Stroganoff

Just before the party: Add vegetables to rice. Bake dip. Prepare avocado garnish for Stroganoff

During the party: Add sour cream to Stroganoff

Hot Green Chile Dip

FOR 16 SERVINGS

We like this best warm, but it may also be served at room temperature.

1	pound fresh mild green chiles (California, Anaheim, or poblano) *or* 2 cans (7 ounces each) whole green chiles, rinsed and seeded
1½	cups mayonnaise
½	cup sour cream (or use an additional ½ cup mayonnaise)
1	small garlic clove, pressed or minced
10	ounces (2¼ cups) freshly grated Parmesan cheese
	Paprika

TO SERVE:

Corn chips *or* an assortment of dippers (directions follow)

Preheat oven to 300°F.

If using fresh chiles, roast and peel them according to directions in Hacienda Brown Rice (page 114).

Add all ingredients except paprika to the container of a blender or food processor, reserving 2 tablespoons of the Parmesan; blend well. Use a rubber spatula to transfer the mixture to a 5- to 6-cup ovenproof serving dish. Sprinkle with reserved Parmesan and a bit of paprika.

Bake for 30 minutes, or until the mixture is bubbly and slightly puffed. Serve hot or at room temperature with your choice of dippers.

To Prepare in Advance: Refrigerate the unbaked dip for up to 48 hours. Bake, adding 5 to 10 minutes to the baking time, just before serving.

Red, Yellow, Green, and Purple Dippers

FOR 16 SERVINGS

You will find yellow bell peppers, as well as some that are almost black, at gourmet produce markets. These varieties make for lively conversation. If, however, red and green are the only choices available, simply buy more of those.

    3   each red, yellow, and green bell peppers
    ½   medium head red cabbage

Stem, seed, and remove membranes from two of each color pepper and cut into strips. Cut the tops off the remaining one of each color pepper to form a cup.

Core the cabbage and cut into thin lengthwise wedges. Select the firmest, thickest pieces to use for dippers.

Stand the pepper strips and cabbage spears in the pepper cups (see photograph) and set near the dip.

To Prepare in Advance: Wrap the pepper cups and vegetable pieces in damp paper towels, seal in plastic bags, and refrigerate for up to 36 hours.

Tortilla Chips

FOR 16 SERVINGS

You may wish to serve these along with or in place of the colorful bell pepper dippers.

    1   dozen corn tortillas
        vegetable oil for frying

Cut the tortillas in eighths and, if fresh, dry them at room temperature for an hour or longer. Heat ¾ inch of oil in a wok or skillet and fry the tortillas, a few at a time, until golden and crisp. Drain well on paper towels.

To Prepare in Advance: These are best served within 2 to 3 hours of cooking, but they may be kept crisp in an airtight container for up to 24 hours.

Southwestern Stroganoff

FOR ABOUT 16 SERVINGS

This is a wonderful buffet dish using leftover turkey or chicken. It is garnished with avocado wedges, sprigs of cilantro, and pomegranate seeds.

10 ounces fresh mild green chiles (California, Anaheim, or poblano), or 2 cans (7 ounces each) whole green chiles, rinsed, seeded, and cut into thin strips
½ cup (1 stick) butter
3 medium-size white onions, minced
3 medium garlic cloves, chopped
¼ cup chili powder
  Pinch of ground cloves
½ cup all-purpose flour
4 cups strong turkey or chicken broth, undiluted if canned (see Note)
1 cup dry vermouth *or* 1¼ cups dry white wine
4 cups shredded cooked turkey breast or chicken
2 cups sour cream

  TO GARNISH AND SERVE:

1 ripe avocado, peeled, pitted, and cut into thin wedges
½ cup chopped cilantro (fresh coriander), optional
  Seeds from ½ ripe pomegranate

Note: If the broth you use is not richly seasoned, flavor the finished Stroganoff to taste with chicken stock base or chicken bouillon cubes.

If using fresh chiles, roast and peel them as directed in the recipe for Hacienda Brown Rice. Cut into thin lengthwise strips.

Melt butter in a heavy pot of at least 6 quarts capacity over medium-high heat. Sauté the onions and garlic for 5 minutes, or until onion is transparent. Stir in the chili powder and cloves and stir for a minute or so, then add the flour. Cook over low heat for about 3 minutes to toast the flour lightly and remove any raw taste. Gradually add the chicken or turkey broth, then the wine and chiles. Bring to a simmer and stir until thickened. Lower the heat and simmer for 10 minutes to evaporate the alcohol.

Add the shredded turkey or chicken and simmer to heat it through. Just before serving, stir sour cream into the hot turkey mixture, but take care that it does not boil or the sour cream will curdle. Transfer to a serving dish and garnish the top of the Stroganoff with the avocado, cilantro, and pomegranate seeds.

To Prepare in Advance: The Stroganoff may be made several days ahead up to the point of adding the turkey or chicken and stored in the refrigerator; it may also be frozen for up to 3 months. Thaw if frozen and reheat in a heavy saucepan or crockpot, stirring in the sour cream within a few minutes of serving. Reheat any leftover Stroganoff in a double boiler over barely simmering water.

Beef Picadillo

FOR 16 SERVINGS
(12 servings if no other main course is offered)

One evening we were invited to a party where a dish that inspired this one was quickly and easily served buffet-style for 50 to 60 guests. Everyone loved it. Picadillo is a traditional Mexican filling for *chiles rellenos* (stuffed chiles) and for *empanadas* (pastry turnovers).

⅓ cup olive oil
3 large onions, minced
3 garlic cloves, pressed or minced
2 green bell peppers, seeds and membranes removed, finely diced
4 pounds lean ground beef
1½ cups dry Sherry
2 cans (15 ounces each) tomato sauce
1 can (12 ounces) tomato paste
1 tablespoon celery salt
2 tablespoons chopped fresh oregano *or* 2 teaspoons dried oregano, crumbled

1 teaspoon freshly ground black pepper
1 teaspoon ground cumin
½ teaspoon cinnamon
    Pinch of ground cloves
1 cup raisins
½ cup drained capers
1½ cups slivered (not sliced) almonds, toasted at 350°F until
        golden

Heat olive oil in heavy large Dutch oven. Stir in onions, garlic, and green peppers and cook, stirring, until onion is soft and transparent.

Add the meat and mash with the back of the spoon until it is crumbly and has lost all red color. Stir in the remaining ingredients except the almonds and simmer uncovered for an hour or so, until the mixture is as thick as chili.

Transfer to a serving dish and sprinkle toasted almonds over the top.

To Prepare in Advance: This freezes beautifully for up to 3 months. Thaw and reheat, adding almonds just before serving.

Fiesta Rice Pilaf

FOR 16 SERVINGS

This is a basic rice pilaf to which we have added some colorful vegetables for a festive touch.

OVEN RICE:

4 cups raw white rice, rinsed with cold water
1 tablespoon salt (if using water or unsalted broth)
1 tablespoon butter
1 teaspoon vinegar or fresh lemon juice
8 cups (2 quarts) boiling water or clear chicken broth (if salted,
        omit salt)

VEGETABLES:

½ cup (1 stick) butter
1½ cups sliced carrot
2 bunches scallions (including some of the green tops), sliced
1 package (10 ounces) frozen peas, thawed
Salt and freshly ground pepper to taste

Preheat oven to 375°F. Place the oven rice ingredients in a large casserole or Dutch oven with a very tight-fitting lid. Bake for 45 minutes. Check to see if the rice is done and the liquid has been absorbed; if necessary, cook a few minutes longer. Remove from the oven and fluff with a fork.

Melt the butter in a skillet and add the vegetables. Cook, covered, for 2 to 3 minutes. Toss with the cooked rice. Taste and correct seasoning.

To Prepare in Advance: The rice may be cooked in the morning, chilled, and reheated in a conventional or microwave oven. Cook the vegetables and stir into the rice within an hour of serving; keep warm.

Buffet Salad Bowl Caesar

FOR 16 SERVINGS

Caesar Salad is a Southwestern specialty created at Caesar's Restaurant in the Mexican border town of Tijuana. This rather unorthodox version holds up well because guests spoon on the dressing when they serve themselves.

CROUTONS (for 2 cups):

½ cup olive oil
8 to 10 slices day-old bread (white, wholewheat, or French), crusts trimmed, cut into ½-inch cubes

CAESAR DRESSING:

2 large garlic cloves, minced
1 can (2 ounces) flat anchovy fillets, rinsed and drained
½ cup fresh lemon juice
4 eggs, simmered in boiling water for 1 minute and cooled

½ cup freshly grated Parmesan cheese
1½ cups light olive oil
Freshly ground black pepper to taste
1½ pounds romaine lettuce, leaves rinsed, dried, and broken into bite-size pieces

To make croutons, heat olive oil in small skillet over medium heat until hot but not smoking. Toss a small handful of cubes into the oil, moving them constantly until evenly browned. Remove with a slotted spoon and drain on paper towels.

To make the dressing, combine garlic, anchovy fillets, and lemon juice in blender or food processor fitted with steel blade. Process briefly and add the 4 coddled eggs and Parmesan. Pour in the oil with the motor running. Season to taste with freshly ground black pepper. Serve in a dish or sauceboat with a ladle.

Place the prepared romaine lettuce in a large salad bowl for guests to serve themselves.

To Prepare in Advance: Croutons may be stored in an airtight container at room temperature for up to a week. The dressing may be refrigerated for up to 24 hours; bring to room temperature and shake or whisk to recombine. The prepared lettuce may be stored, wrapped in damp paper towels, in a plastic bag in the refrigerator for up to 24 hours as well. Transfer to a salad bowl just before serving.

Jicama, Cucumber, and Orange Salad

FOR 16 SERVINGS

This is one version of the popular Mexican salad, *Pico de Gallo* (beak of the rooster).

1½ pounds jicama, peeled and cubed (about 3 cups) (see Note)
1 hothouse cucumber (this need not be peeled or seeded)
3 navel oranges, peeled and cubed
⅓ cup fresh lime juice
1 teaspoon chili powder
¼ teaspoon salt

Note: Jicama is a tropical root vegetable related to morning glory that looks very much like a brown-skinned turnip. Its crisp white flesh tastes like a delicious cross between an apple and a water chestnut. You will find it in many super-markets nowadays; it is sold whole or in pieces with plastic wrap covering the cut surfaces.

Combine all ingredients except salt in a glass or stainless steel bowl and chill for at least 2 hours. Sprinkle with salt, toss and serve.

To Prepare in Advance: Omit salt and refrigerate, covered, up to 3 days. Salt just before serving.

Lime Meringue Pie with Toasted Nut Crust

MAKES ONE 9-INCH PIE, SERVING 8
(make 2 pies for 16 servings)

This has a wonderful Margarita-like flavor.

TOASTED NUT CRUST:

1½ cups (6 ounces) ground pecans, Brazil nuts, or walnuts
¼ cup sugar
¼ teaspoon cinnamon
2 tablespoons (¼ stick) unsalted butter

LIME FILLING:

1½ cups sugar
½ cup cornstarch
   Pinch of salt
1⅔ cups cold water
4 egg yolks, lightly beaten
⅔ cup fresh lime juice
2 tablespoons (¼ stick) unsalted butter
1 teaspoon grated lime rind

MERINGUE:

6 egg whites
¼ teaspoon cream of tartar
¼ teaspoon salt
¼ cup sugar
½ teaspoon vanilla

TO GARNISH:

1 teaspoon grated lime rind

To make the crust, preheat the oven to 400°F. Combine crust ingredients and press into the bottom and sides of a 9-inch piepan. Bake for 6 minutes; remove from oven and cool to room temperature.

For the lime filling, mix together the sugar, cornstarch, and salt in a heavy saucepan. Gradually whisk in the water, place over medium heat, and cook, stirring constantly, until thickened and smooth. Beat the egg yolks in a small mixing bowl. Whisk in about ¼ cup of the cornstarch mixture, then pour the yolk mixture into the saucepan and cook over very low heat, stirring constantly, for 2 minutes, taking care that the mixture does not boil. Remove from the heat and add the lime juice, butter, and lime rind. Pour the filling into the prepared nut crust.

Lower the oven temperature to 350°F and prepare the meringue topping while the filling is still warm. Beat the egg whites in a clean mixing bowl until foamy. Add the cream of tartar and salt and beat at medium speed, adding the sugar a tablespoon at a time, beating well after each addition. Once all the sugar has been added, beat in the vanilla. Turn the mixer to high speed and beat until the meringue is very stiff—the peaks will stand straight when the beaters are lifted.

Spoon half the meringue onto the *warm* lime filling (this prevents shrinking), spreading it to touch the crust on all sides. Mound the remaining meringue in the middle, forming peaks with a spatula as you do so. Bake in the center of the oven for 15 minutes, or until peaks are golden brown. Remove from oven, sprinkle grated lime peel over top, and let cool at room temprature for 2 hours before slicing.

To Prepare in Advance: The nut crust may be baked and refrigerated for up to 3 days. Make the lime filling and meringue within 8 hours of serving. Do not refrigerate the finished pie or the meringue will "weep".

W I N T E R

THE cold days of winter call for hearty and comforting food, crackling fires, and just plain coziness. Now we enjoy the warmth of our kitchen and a steaming mug of "Saturday Soup," a ritual brew made from all the pieces of vegetables and bones saved up for this purpose during the week. It is over this that we are likely to plan our winter revelries.

The produce section now is full potatoes and other root vegetables, including celery root (which is delicious in soups), leeks, fennel, and cabbages, including the very extravagant looking, but delicately flavored, Savoy cabbage. We have a penchant for dishes that simmer all day and smell up the house deliciously—baked beans and such—and their goodness only improves on waiting a day or two before reheating. Pat Crowleys's Brisket in Red Wine is just such a dish and will be good for New Year's.

We always look forward to the holidays, vowing each year to make them fresh for ourselves and our friends, to let go of old expectations. A Trim-the-Tree supper would be fun and easy. We'll welcome guests with spiced and spiked cider and decorate the tree together. Today's soup is so good that we can plan our menu around it as a main course. For New Year's Day we'll ask some friends to come and watch the games, and set out a buffet that hardly needs tending at all. Both these menus can be prepared well ahead of time and involve very little last minute flurry.

Because it's cold it doesn't mean we won't still enjoy the outdoors this season. A day of cross-country skiing and bird and animal watching, followed by a hearty take-along supper with friends at their cabin by the lake, will exemplify what winter is all about: the crunch of skis against the snow, while all the rest is silence. We'll collect pine cones to decorate the house.

And what could be cozier or more comforting than to stay in a warm bed on one cold morning in the middle of February, and wake up to breakfast brought on a tray. It's a great way to celebrate Valentine's Day, and love, which creates all good things.

AN AFTER-SKI SUPPER
(FOR 6)

"Hot Apple Pie"
Assorted Nuts in the Shell

Oven Raclette
Boiled Red Potatoes
Pickled Onions and Cornichons

Crusty French Rolls

Broccoli with Olive Oil and Garlic★

Pepper Nuts

Tangerines

Coffee with Tuaca Liqueur

★See Index

AN AFTER-SKI SUPPER

Here is a menu to enjoy with friends after an invigorating day in the snow. Whether your group has been skiing, hiking, or building snowmen, this bracing winter day will bring exertion, and therefore hearty appetites.

While everyone is getting out of their mittens, boots, parkas, hats, and earmuffs, offer them a ski-resort drink called Hot Apple Pie to warm them in a hurry. The rest of the meal can be leisurely as you sit in front of a roaring fire, cracking nuts in the shell, to replenish the energy lost to the cold.

Of course this menu can be served on any frosty day, in a mountain cabin or at home. And who should know better than the Swiss how to celebrate winter? Our easy main course is a simple version of their national dish, melted cheese on hot plates served with boiled red potatoes, pickled onions, and tiny *cornichon* pickles. Broccoli, which is abundant in the markets now, makes a colorful accompaniment, as do crusty French rolls to use for dipping in the melted cheese.

Dessert is simple, some seasonal tangerines and cookies, followed, perhaps, by steaming coffee spiked with a bit of Tuaca liqueur.

SHOPPING LIST

12	small red potatoes
10	to 12 tangerines
1	apple
2	pounds cheese for raclette (Bagnes, Jarlsberg, Monterey Jack, Muenster, Fontina, or a combination)
½	cup (4 ounces) heavy cream
12	crusty French rolls
½	cup chopped pecans or walnuts
	Assorted nuts in the shell
1½	quarts (48 ounces) apple cider
8	to 10 ounces Tuaca liqueur
1	cup pickled onions
1	cup *cornichons*

Staples

1 egg
All-purpose flour (1½ cups)
Sugar (⅓ cup)
Dark brown sugar (⅓ cup)
Powdered sugar (about ¼ cup)
Almonds (2 tablespoons ground)
Baking soda (½ teaspoon)
Whole nutmeg, to grate
Whole cloves (6)
Cinnamon (¾ teaspoon)
Cloves (¼ teaspoon)
Allspice (¼ teaspoon)
Black pepper (¼ teaspoon)
Cardamom (¼ teaspoon)
Vanilla (1 teaspoon)

DO-AHEAD TIMETABLE

Up to a month ahead: Make Pepper Nuts

Up to three days ahead: Cook broccoli

Day of the party: Whip cream

Just before the party: Cook potatoes. Slice cheese

During the party: Make drinks and top with whipped cream. Heat French bread. Slice cheese and heat; garnish. Sprinkle cookies with powdered sugar

"Hot Apple Pie"

FOR 6 SERVINGS

The recipe for this splendidly warming winter drink was brought to us from the ski slopes at Lake Tahoe by our friend Candace Kommers.

1½	quarts (48 ounces) apple cider (not hard cider)
6	whole cloves
¼	teaspoon cinnamon
¾	cup (6 ounces) Tuaca liqueur (see Note)

TO GARNISH AND SERVE:

½	cup heavy cream, whipped to soft peaks
	Freshly grated nutmeg

Note: Tuaca is an Italian liqueur with a nice vanilla and almond overtone. It is available in well-stocked liquor stores. We enjoy it in after-dinner coffee, too.

Bring the cider, cloves, and cinnamon to a simmer in a small saucepan, cover, and cook over low heat for 10 minutes. Remove from heat and stir in the Tuaca. Ladle into warm mugs. Top each serving with a generous dollop of whipped cream and a sprinkling of nutmeg.

 *Oven Raclette*

FOR 6 SERVINGS

The national dish of Switzerland is not fondue but raclette, made by placing half a wheel of Bagnes (a Swiss-type cheese with good melting properties) in front of a roaring fire until the surface melts, and then scraping the melted part onto warm plates to serve with small boiled red potatoes, pickled onions, and sweet gherkins or *cornichons* (available at gourmet specialty shops). We make an easier version by melting sliced cheese in individual ovenproof dishes.

2   pounds mellow-flavored cheese with good melting properties
    (Jarlsberg, Monterey Jack, Muenster, Fontina, *or* a
    combination)

TO SERVE:

12 small red potatoes, boiled and kept hot
    Pickled onions
    Cornichons
    Crusty French rolls, warmed

Preheat the oven to 400°F. Cut the cheese into even slices about ½ inch thick and place on metal platters or heatproof dishes. Bake until the cheese is melted. Serve immediately with boiled potatoes, onions, cornichons, and warmed French rolls.

 *Pepper Nuts*

FOR ABOUT 4 DOZEN COOKIES

Pfeffernüsse is the German name for a pepper-flavored cookie that is called Pepparnotter in Sweden and Pebernodder in Denmark, and that is traditionally served during the winter holidays. Our version omits the traditional candied rinds. These cookies improve on aging, which makes them ideal for traveling.

1	egg
⅓	cup firmly packed dark brown sugar
⅓	cup sugar
2	tablespoons ground almonds
½	teaspoon cinnamon
¼	teaspoon ground cloves
¼	teaspoon ground allspice
⅛	teaspoon ground cardamom
¼	teaspoon freshly ground black pepper
1½	cups sifted all-purpose flour
½	teaspoon baking soda
	a piece of apple to place in the tin while the cookies age
	powdered sugar (garnish)

In the large bowl of an electric mixer beat the egg with the brown and white sugar until thick and fluffy. Add the almonds and spices and mix well.

Sift flour with baking soda and add to the flour mixture—the dough will be stiff. Form into a log about 1-inch in diameter, wrap in plastic wrap or foil, and refrigerate for 2 to 3 days so the flavors will fully develop.

Preheat oven to 300°F and place rack in center postion. Butter a large baking sheet. Cut crosswise slices of dough about ¾-inch thick and place, cut side flat, on baking sheet. Bake for 20 minutes or so until lightly browned. Remove from baking sheet and cool completely. Roll in powdered sugar before serving.

To Prepare in Advance: These are best when aged for at least a week in an air-tight tin with a slice of apple.

A TRIM-THE-TREE GET-TOGETHER
(FOR 10 TO 12)

Warming Holiday Punch Bowl

Caramel Nut Corn

Italian Sausage Soup

Parmesan Bread Wreath

Apple and Fennel Salad

Marzipan Torte

Hot Coffee
with Assorted Liqueurs

A Trim-the-Tree Get-Together

Trimming the tree is a perfect excuse to have a party. New friends, old friends, friends of friends, each and all are welcome, but we have one stipulation: they have to bring an ornament for the Christmas tree. We get some pretty fancy stuff that way.

Both children and adults love this kind of party. We have big baskets of Caramel Nut Corn all over, just to keep the energy up, and of course a holiday punch bowl to keep the grownups smiling.

We usually get some helping hands in assembling the buffet, but there's no big hurry. The food featured here will look good all evening. We put on some Christmas carols, replenish the store of caramel corn and the contents of the punch bowl, and take Polaroid pictures as if this were a spread for a national magazine. It's not—we later give them away to our guests.

Finally the tree is lit and everyone has placed an ornament on it. The buffet, decorated with pine boughs and red apples that have been hollowed to hold votive candles, now has our full attention. The main course is a robust Italian Sausage Soup with orzo, a rice-shaped pasta, and a lovely wreath of bread flavored with olive oil, garlic, and Parmesan and decorated with strips of peeled red peppers. Our seasonal salad contains crisp red apples and fennel, a slightly licorice-tasting, celery-like bulb. Dessert is a torte with a subtle marzipan flavor and light texture.

We've all participated in the evening, feel comfortable with one another, and have a wonderful time: a perfect beginning to the holiday season. Later, as guests leave, we give them each a small wrapped present for under their own trees.

SHOPPING LIST

Fresh fruit to serve with torte (optional)

3 red Delicious or McIntosh apples (for salad)

Apples (to hold candles for table centerpiece)

2 medium onions

4 carrots

4 zucchini or 8 ounces green beans

2 green bell peppers

2 red bell peppers or 1 jar (4 ounces) sliced pimientos

Fresh basil (2 tablespoons minced)

Fresh oregano (1 tablespoon minced)

Fresh parsley

2 large oranges

2 fennel bulbs or 1 celery heart

3 lemons (for juice and grated rind)

2 pounds Italian sausage (hot, sweet, or a combination)

5 ounces Parmesan cheese

8 eggs

6 sticks butter

1 cup (8 ounces) heavy cream

1 cup cake flour

2 packages (7 ounces each) almond paste

1 cup orzo (rice-shaped pasta) or substitute

½ cup unpopped popcorn

2 cans (28 ounces each) crushed tomatoes in tomato puree

10 cups chicken broth

1 pound French or Italian bread ring or, if unavailable, a long loaf

2 cups pecan halves

1½ cups unblanched almonds

½ cup shelled hazelnuts or unsalted peanuts

3 quarts apple cider

2 cups (one 500-ml bottle) golden rum

1 cup dry vermouth, white wine, or red wine

¼ cup Grand Marnier

Liqueurs to serve with coffee

Votive candles

Staples

Garlic (6 cloves)

Olive oil (about 1½ cups)

Vegetable oil (3 tablespoons)

Red wine vinegar (1 tablespoon)

Dijon mustard (1½ teaspoons)

Worcestershire sauce (½ teaspoon)

Almond extract (½ teaspoons)

Vanilla (1½ teaspoons)

Light corn syrup (½ cup)

Sugar (3 cups)

All-purpose flour (1½ cups)

Powdered sugar (2 to 3 tablespoons)

Baking powder (¾ teaspoon)

Dried basil (2 teaspoons, if fresh not available)

Dried oregano (1 teaspoon, if
   fresh not available)
Allspice berries (1 tablespoon)
Cinnamon stick (1)
Salt
Black pepper

From the yard or Christmas tree lot

Pine boughs for centerpiece
Holly leaves, without toxic
   berries

DO-AHEAD TIMETABLE

Up to a month ahead: Make caramel-nut corn. Prepare soup and freeze. Bake
   marzipan torte and freeze

Up to a week ahead: Make dressing for apple salad

Up to three days ahead: Cook broccoli. Make base for punch

Two days ahead: Prepare ham, cheese, and chile dip

Day before the party; Thaw soup. Thaw torte

Day of the party: Assemble bread wreath. Cut and fill sourdough bread,
   wrap in foil

Just before the party: Bake sourdough with dip (2 hours ahead). Heat punch
   and add rum. Toss apple and fennel salad. Make coffee

During the party: Bake bread wreath

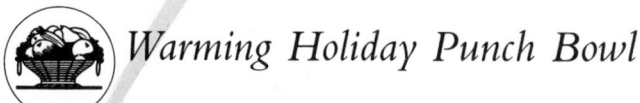

Warming Holiday Punch Bowl

FOR 4 QUARTS
(for 12 servings with seconds)

We use an enamel-on-steel stockpot to make this, and serve it directly from the stove.

    3   quarts apple cider
   ½   cup sugar
    2   large oranges, washed and cut crosswise into ¼-inch slices
    2   lemons, washed and cut crosswise into ¼-inch slices
    1   tablespoon whole allspice berries
    1   cinnamon stick
    2   cups (one 500-ml bottle) golden rum

In a large pot combine cider, sugar, fruit, and spices. Cover and simmer slowly for 1 hour. Strain. Add the rum and heat thoroughly, but do not boil. Serve hot.

To Prepare in Advance: The basic mixture without rum may be simmered several days in advance. Just before serving, reheat, add rum, and serve hot.

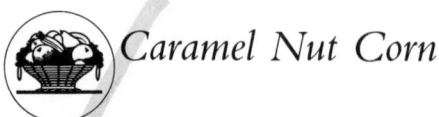

Caramel Nut Corn

MAKES ABOUT 3 QUARTS

This is a favorite wintertime snack.

    3   tablespoons vegetable oil
   ½   cup unpopped popcorn
    2   cups pecan halves
1½   cups unblanched almonds
   ½   cup shelled hazelnuts or unsalted peanuts
1¼   cups sugar

1   cup (2 sticks) butter
½   cup light corn syrup
1½ teaspoons vanilla

Heat the oil in a heavy saucepan of at least 4 quarts capacity and pop the popcorn according to package directions. Set aside.

Toast the nuts on a baking sheet at 350°F for about 15 minutes, or until well browned. If using hazelnuts, rub them with a towel after toasting to remove some (but not all) of their dark skins.

Oil a large roasting pan or rimmed baking sheet. Place the nuts and popcorn in it and mix well.

In a small heavy saucepan combine the sugar, butter, and corn syrup. Cook without stirring until the mixture turns a golden caramel color (about 265°F on a candy thermometer). Remove from heat and stir in the vanilla. Pour the caramel over the popcorn mixture and stir to coat evenly. Bake in a 350°F oven for 15 minutes, stirring every 5 minutes. Remove from the oven and let cool, stirring every 5 minutes to coat evenly with the liquid caramel, until the mixture begins to set. Turn out of the pan onto buttered foil and let cool completely.

Break into serving pieces.

To Prepare in Advance: Store in plastic bags inside airtight containers for up to a month.

Italian Sausage Soup

FOR 10 TO 12 SERVINGS

Everyone raves about this hearty, home-style soup!

2   pounds Italian sausage—hot, sweet, or a combination
4   carrots, peeled
4   zucchini, *or* 8 ounces green beans
2   green bell peppers, seeds and membranes removed
2   medium onions, finely chopped
2   garlic cloves, minced
1   cup dry vermouth, dry white wine, *or* red wine

10 cups chicken broth

2 cans (28 ounces each) crushed tomatoes in tomato puree

2 tablespoons minced fresh basil, *or* 2 teaspoons dried basil, crumbled

1 tablespoon minced fresh oregano, *or* 1 teaspoon dried oregano, crumbled

Salt and freshly ground black pepper to taste

1 cup uncooked orzo (see Note 2)

TO SERVE:

1¼ cups (5 ounces) freshly grated Parmesan cheese

Note 1: Canned tomatoes, especially in wintertime, are often the cook's best bet for dishes that will be cooked. Their flavor is often far superior to that of fresh tomatoes in the markets, and they are very convenient. "Peeled crushed tomatoes with added puree" may be used in place of the "peeled whole tomatoes with their liquid" called for in most recipes. Read the labels of canned tomatoes to avoid added acid, calcium salts, and sugar.

Note 2: Orzo is a rice-shaped pasta. If unavailable, substitute another small pasta, such as tubettini.

Remove the casings from the sausage and discard. Brown the sausage in a heavy Dutch oven or large saucepan, mashing it with the back of a spoon until the meat is no longer pink and it has rendered most of its fat.

Meanwhile, finely dice the carrots, zucchini or green beans, and bell peppers. (If using a food processor, cut the carrots and pepper into 1-inch pieces and process with the steel blade using on-off bursts until chopped. Add the zucchini, also cut into 1-inch pieces, and process a few more bursts.)

Spoon out most of the fat from the cooked sausage and discard. Add the onions and garlic and cook, stirring, until soft but not browned. Add all remaining ingredients except orzo and bring to a boil. When the soup is boiling, add the orzo and continue cooking for 20 minutes. Serve in heavy soup bowls. Let guests sprinkle Parmesan over each serving.

To Prepare in Advance: Like most hearty soups, this tastes best if it is cooled, refrigerated overnight, then reheated to serve.

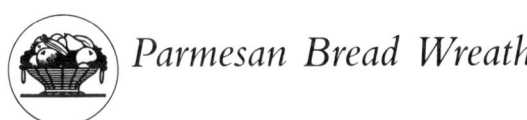

Parmesan Bread Wreath

FOR AT LEAST 12 SERVINGS

1	French or Italian bread ring (1 pound) (see Note)
¾	cup olive oil
2	medium garlic cloves, minced or pressed
¾	cup freshly grated Parmesan cheese
2	red bell peppers, roasted and peeled, seeds and membranes removed (see Torta d'Alba recipe, page 15) *or* 1 jar (4 ounces) sliced pimientos, drained

TO GARNISH AND SERVE:

2	tablespoons minced fresh parsley
	Holly leaves (without toxic berries), rinsed

Note: These are easy to find in California supermarkets. If not available, substitute a 1-pound loaf of French bread.

Preheat oven to 425°F. Cut the bread ring in half crosswise, forming two rings. Combine the olive oil and garlic, mixing until well blended. Add the Parmesan and peeled red peppers or pimientos and spread the mixture evenly over the cut side of both bread rings.

Bake for about 20 minutes, or until the topping is lightly browned. (If it isn't browned to your liking, slide the bread rings under the broiler for a few seconds—but don't forget to watch them.) Sprinkle with parsley and cut each round into 10 pieces, leaving ring shape intact for serving. Garnish the serving dish with holly.

To Prepare in Advance: Assemble the bread rings in the morning and refrigerate. Bake just before serving.

Apple and Fennel Salad

FOR 10 TO 12 SERVINGS

2 fennel bulbs (if not available substitute 1 celery heart)
2 tablespoons fresh lemon juice
3 medium-size red Delicious or McIntosh apples
½ recipe Mustard Vinaigrette (page 18)

Remove and discard tough outer stalks from fennel. Cut the hearts into thin slices. Place in a bowl of ice water to which you have added 2 tablespoons lemon juice. Core the apples, cut into thin wedges, and add them to the acidulated water with the fennel. Refrigerate 1 hour.

Drain fennel and apples, blot dry, and toss with mustard vinaigrette. Decorate, if desired, with the leafy dill-like fronds of the fennel stalks.

To Prepare in Advance: Mustard vinaigrette, except for the addition of beaten egg white, keeps for weeks in the refrigerator. Prepare the fennel and apples in the morning and leave in lemon water in the refrigerator until one hour before serving. Proceed as directed.

Marzipan Torte

FOR 10 TO 12 SERVINGS

At Wolfgang Puck's innovative Los Angeles restaurant, Spago, pastry chef Nancy Silverton makes a marvelous moist almond dessert topped with a layer of puff pastry. We top our own version with sweetened whipped cream and the most beautiful fresh fruit we can find.

A 9-inch springform pan completely lined with Sweet Tart Pastry

ALMOND FILLING:

2   packages (7 ounces each) almond paste
1   cup (2 sticks) unsalted butter, at room temperature
1   cup sugar
    Rind of 2 to 3 lemons, minced
¼   cup Grand Marnier
½   teaspoon almond extract
6   eggs
1   cup cake flour
¾   teaspoon baking powder

TO GARNISH AND SERVE:

Powdered sugar, sifted through a strainer
1   cup heavy cream, whipped and sweetened with 2 to 3 table-
        spoons powdered sugar
    Fresh fruit, whole or cut up, as available

Adjust rack to center of oven and preheat to 350°F. Make the tart pastry and line the pan as the recipe directs. Bake for 25 minutes.

Meanwhile, using electric mixer, cream together the almond paste, butter, and sugar until well blended and smooth. Add the lemon rind, Grand Marnier, and almond extract and continue beating. Beat in eggs one at a time, beating well after each addition.

Blend flour and baking powder into almond paste mixture. Turn batter into pastry-lined pan (it is not necessary to cool pastry before filling with batter). Bake for 70 to 75 minutes. Cover the top of the cake with foil to prevent over-browning and continue baking for 30 minutes longer, or until a toothpick inserted in the middle comes out clean. Let cool at least 20 minutes before removing the sides of the pan.

Sprinkle with powdered sugar. Serve torte warm or at room temperature with whipped cream and fresh fruit.

To Prepare in Advance: Store in the refrigerator for up to 3 days or freeze for up to 3 months. Thaw at room temperature.

A NEW YEAR'S DAY
WATCH-THE-GAME BUFFET
(FOR 10 TO 12)

Open Bar

Hot Brie Fondue with Caraway Seed and Lahvosh

Pat Crowley's Brisket of Beef Braised in Red Wine

Torte Lyonnaise

Pea and Cauliflower Slaw

Hazelnut Cheesecake

Hot Coffee

A NEW YEAR'S DAY WATCH-THE-GAME BUFFET

Here is a good menu with which to celebrate the New Year: The best part about it is that it needs very little attention from you. All the food holds up beautifully at room temperature or on a warming tray, so it will be perfect for drop-in guests. And on New Year's Day, that can happen any time.

A welcoming snack is delicious warm Brie, served like a cheese fondue for dipping with broken pieces of Armenian cracker bread *(lahvosh)*. Guests can serve themselves from an open bar. We suggest wines, liquors and mixes, including do-it-yourself Bloody Marys, and lots of hot coffee (for those who may have celebrated a bit too much already).

At halftime, or whenever hunger strikes, everyone can help himself to slices of brisket with a tangy red wine and pureed vegetable sauce, a warm slice of Torte Lyonnaise (puff pastry-encased potatoes flavored with garlic, chives, and cream), and a crisp Pea and Cauliflower Slaw.

Dessert is a creamy Hazelnut Cheesecake that has the rich flavor of the toasted nuts throughout. It's wonderful with coffee.

SHOPPING LIST

6 pounds russet (baking) potatoes
5 medium onions
1 head garlic
1 bunch scallions
1 head cauliflower
   Fresh mixed herbs (tarragon,
      chervil, thyme, marjoram—1
      tablespoon total)
   Fresh parsley
   Fresh dill (1 tablespoon
      snipped)
   Lemons and limes (for bar use)
1 lemon (for grated rind and 2
      tablespoons juice)
   A 5-pound lean beef brisket
   A 2-pound round of French
      Brie cheese
2 pounds cream cheese
8 eggs
2 sticks butter
1 cup (8 ounces) heavy cream
2½ pounds fresh or 2 packages
      (17¼ ounces each) frozen
      puff pastry
2 packages (10 ounces each) or
      one 20-ounce bag frozen
      tiny peas
   Armenian cracker bread
      (lahvosh) or other sturdy,
      crisp crackers
2¼ cups shelled hazelnuts
1 bottle (750 ml) red Burgundy
¼ cup Port wine
   Liquor for an open bar
   Mixers
   Ice

Staples

   Mayonnaise (1 cup)
   Olive oil (6 tablespoons)
   Tomato paste (¼ cup)
   Dijon mustard (1 tablespoon)
   Worcestershire sauce (1
      tablespoon)
   Sugar (1¾ cups)
   Herbes de Provence (1 teaspoon,
      if fresh herbs not available)
   Caraway seed (2 teaspoons)
   Seasoned salt
   Salt
   Black or white pepper

DO-AHEAD TIMETABLE

Up to a month ahead: Bake and freeze cheesecake

Up to three days ahead: Bake brisket. Make slaw

One day ahead: Assemble Tortes Lyonnaise

Day of the party: Slice brisket and assemble with sauce in baking dish

Just before the party: Set out ice on bar. Prepare Brie for baking. Bake Tortes
      Lyonnaise

During the party: Bake Brie

 # Hot Brie Fondue with Caraway Seed and Lahvosh

FOR 12 OR MORE APPETIZER SERVINGS

Brie has a fondue-like consistency when melted, perfect to serve with unseasoned crackers for dipping. The cheese needn't be perfectly ripened; in fact, it should be slightly underripe for this purpose.

A 2-pound round of French Brie
2 teaspoons caraway seed

TO SERVE:

Armenian cracker bread *(lahvosh) or* other sturdy, crisp
crackers of your choice

Preheat the oven to 475°F. Heat the caraway seeds over medium heat in a small dry skillet just until you begin to smell their fragrance—this will bring out their full flavor. Turn out of the pan and set aside. Place the chilled cheese in a ceramic quiche dish or ovenproof serving dish just large enough to hold it. Bake until the cheese feels soft and starts to burst its rind, about 10 minutes.

Using a narrow spatula, lift off and discard the top rind of the cheese to reveal the fondue-like interior. Sprinkle the toasted caraway seed over the surface of the cheese and serve with broken pieces of lahvosh for dipping. The hot serving dish will keep the Brie melted and spreadable for at least 30 minutes, or longer if placed on an electric hot tray.

To Prepare in Advance: Leftover cheese may be reheated to serve within 2 to 3 days.

Pat Crowley's Brisket of Beef Braised in Red Wine

FOR 10 TO 12 SERVINGS

Actress Pat Crowley is a good friend and a superb cook. She is such a confident and self-assured lady that she offers last-minute invitations like, "Hey, come on over for dinner. It's just the family but we've got lots." The red wine sauce for her brisket, thickened with pureed onions and garlic instead of flour, is a real winner.

	A 5-pound lean beef brisket
	Seasoned salt
5	medium onions, chopped
3	garlic cloves, minced or pressed
1	bottle (750 ml) red Burgundy
1	cup water
3 to 4	tablespoons tomato paste
1	tablespoon Worcestershire sauce
	Salt and black pepper to taste

Preheat the oven to 500°F.

Sprinkle the brisket generously with seasoned salt and place it, fat side up, in a heavy roasting pan or kettle that can go into the oven. Roast uncovered for 25 to 35 minutes, or until browned. Sprinkle the onions evenly over the top of the meat. Stir together the garlic, Burgundy, water, tomato paste, and Worcestershire sauce. Pour the liquid around the meat and cover the pan. Lower the oven temperature to 325°F and continue cooking for 4 hours or longer, until very tender.

Lift the meat from the liquid and allow to rest for 20 minutes before slicing. Meanwhile, use a slotted spoon to transfer the onions to a blender or food mill, reserving all the pan juices. Process to a smooth sauce, adding just enough of the reserved liquid to thin to the desired consistency. (Any unused liquid can be sipped as a delicious soup.)

To serve, carve the meat, not too thinly, across the grain. Arrange the slices on a warm platter and spoon sauce over them to coat evenly. Serve extra sauce on the side.

To Prepare in Advance: This recipe may be cooked several days ahead. Cool the meat to room temperature, wrap, and refrigerate. It may be sliced when cold, arranged in a serving dish, and covered with sauce. Reheat at 325°F for about 45 minutes, or until hot.

Torte Lyonnaise

FOR 6 TO 8 SERVINGS
(make two for 12 to 16 servings)

We first tasted a similar dish at Piret's Restaurant in San Diego and could hardly wait to recreate it at home. It is much lighter than it sounds.

FILLING:

3 pounds russet potatoes, scrubbed and baked at 450°F for 45 minutes or until tender
6 tablespoons (¾ stick) butter, melted
½ cup heavy cream
½ cup minced fresh parsley
3 garlic cloves, minced
1 tablespoon minced fresh herbs, such as tarragon, chervil, thyme, and marjoram, *or* 1 teaspoon dried herb blend, such as *Herbes de Provence*
1 teaspoon salt
¼ teaspoon freshly ground black or white pepper

1¼ pounds fresh puff pastry *or* 1 package (17¼ ounces) frozen puff pastry
1 egg, beaten

To make the filling, halve the potatoes lengthwise and scoop the insides into a mixing bowl. Mix in the butter, cream, parsley, garlic, herbs, and seasonings, taking care not to break up the potatoes any more than necessary; the mixture should contain large lumps of potato, which will give it texture. Set aside to cool.
Preheat the oven to 425°F and place the rack in the lowest postion.

185

If using bakery pastry, divide it into two portions, reserving a piece of dough the size of a ping-pong ball for making decorations. If using frozen, remove the two sheets of pastry from the package and allow to thaw for 15 minutes at room temperature. Place one sheet of pastry on an ungreased baking sheet; roll and trim to make a 10½-inch circle (reserve trimmings to cut into shapes for decorating the top of the torte, if desired; see photograph).

Mound the potato filling in the center of the pastry round, leaving a ½-inch border. Brush the border of the pastry with beaten egg.

Roll and trim the remaining sheet of pastry into an 11-inch circle. Place over the top of the potatoes. Fold the edges of the bottom pastry over the edges of the top pastry and seal by pressing with a fork or fingertips. Brush the top of the pastry with beaten egg. The pastry scraps may be cut into decorations, placed on top of the torte, and brushed with egg as well. Make 6 slashes about 1½ inches from the center in the top pastry to allow steam to escape during baking.

Bake for about 25 to 30 minutes, or until golden brown. Slide the torte onto a flat serving dish. Serve warm or at room temperature, cut into wedges.

To Prepare in Advance: The unbaked torte may be refrigerated for up to 24 hours *if the potatoes were cold when the torte was assembled* (this will eliminate the possibility of bacterial growth). Brush with egg wash and bake when desired. The baked torte is best the day it is made, and it suffers from refrigeration. If necessary, leave it uncovered at room temperature for up to 6 hours and reheat at 300°F for about 20 minutes, or until warmed through.

Pea and Cauliflower Slaw

FOR 12 TO 16 SERVINGS

This is fresh tasting, colorful, and very quick to make. Fresh dill can be found in markets most of the year.

- 2 packages (10 ounces each) *or* one 20-ounce bag frozen tiny peas, thawed
- 1 head cauliflower, broken into florets and thinly sliced
- ½ cup sliced scallions

DRESSING:

1   cup mayonnaise *or* yogurt
6   tablespoons Mustard Vinaigrette (page 18) *or* your favorite
        vinaigrette–type salad dressing
1   tablespoon snipped fresh dill
    Salt and freshly ground pepper to taste

Combine the slaw ingredients in a mixing bowl. Stir together the dressing ingredients and pour over the slaw.

This looks beautiful in a glass serving dish. Garnish the top as desired with a tomato rose, nasturtiums, or other nontoxic flowers.

To Prepare in Advance: This salad keeps well in the refrigerator for up to 4 days.

Hazelnut Cheesecake

FOR 12 SERVINGS

This highly addictive dessert is our adaptation of an idea of James Beard's, who was a fellow Guest Lecturer on a trip to Alaska on Princess Cruise Lines. You will find this a delicious item to have on hand in your freezer throughout the holidays to use as an emergency dessert.

2   cups (8 ounces) shelled hazelnuts
2   pounds cream cheese, at room temperature
    Grated rind of 1 lemon
1¾   cups sugar
4   eggs
¼   cup Port
6   halved hazelnuts, to garnish

Toast the hazelnuts on a baking sheet in a preheated 350°F oven for 15 minutes, stirring once or twice. Transfer the nuts to a towel, and while they are still warm, rub off any of the dark outer skin that comes off easily.

Reserve ½ cup of the nuts to garnish the finished cheesecake. Place the remaining 1½ cups in a food processor or blender. Process until coarsely chopped (pieces can be uneven). Set aside about ⅓ of the crushed nuts to garnish the cake.

Beat the cream cheese with the lemon rind (preferably with an electric mixer) until very smooth, scraping the sides of the bowl often with a rubber spatula. Gradually beat in the sugar, followed by the eggs, adding them one at a time and beating well after each addition. Beat in the Port. Fold in the crushed hazelnuts, except those reserved for garnish.

Preheat the oven to 300°F. Butter an 8-inch springform pan and set it on a baking sheet for ease of handling. Turn the cheesecake batter into the springform, smoothing the top. Bake for 1½ to 1¾ hours, or until golden and dry to the touch. Remove from the oven and cool on a rack at room temperature (the cake will shrink considerably during the cooling).

When cool, remove the side of the pan and turn the cake upside down onto a plain or doily-lined serving plate. Sprinkle with the reserved crushed hazelnuts and make a ring of halved hazelnuts on top.

This may be served chilled or at room temperature. For ease in serving, dip your knife into hot water between cuts.

To Prepare in Advance: Store in refrigerator for up to 5 days or in freezer up to 3 months.

VALENTINE'S DAY BREAKFAST IN BED
(FOR 2)

Amaretto Rendezvous

Grapefruit or Cantaloupe Baskets
Filled with Fresh Fruit

Boiled, Poached, or Scrambled Eggs

Gram's Chocolate Cinnamon Rolls

VALENTINE'S DAY BREAKFAST IN BED

February 14 is the day for lovers, and what better way to celebrate than to start the day with a romantic surprise breakfast in bed for you and your sweetheart?

Serve it on trays with placemats and napkins: brand new red and white dishtowels in varied graphic patterns. Begin with coconut-pineapple juice flavored with Amaretto di Saronno, the Italian liqueur known as the drink of love. (Saint Valentine, the patron of lovers, was a Roman. Romeo and Juliet were from Verona. It seems only fitting.) Most strawberries are naturally heart-shaped, so use one to garnish the side of each glass.

You may want to splurge on out-of-season fruits to fill a cantaloupe or grapefruit for such a special occasion. A doily underneath will make it look like a Valentine card. You can assemble it the night before, or put the fruit together quickly as you brew coffee and prepare eggs the way you like them.

You'll have to plan ahead, though, to make the cinnamon rolls, because they require two risings plus baking. They can be baked ahead and frozen for this and other occasions.

Everything in place? Don't forget the card.

SHOPPING LIST

1 large grapefruit or
  medium cantaloupe
  Fresh fruits in season to
  fill grapefruit or
  cantaloupe (orange,
  melon, berries, kiwi,
  pomegranate)
2 heart-shaped strawberries
  (optional)
2 mint sprigs
5 to 6 eggs
2 sticks butter
¼ cup cream or milk
1 package active dry yeast
½ cup miniature semisweet
  chocolate chips

½ cup chopped walnuts or
  pecans
1½ cups (12 ounces) bottled
  pineapple-coconut juice
  (without added sugar)
½ cup (4 ounces) Amaretto
  di Saronno liqueur

Staples

All-purpose flour (2¼
  cups)
Powdered sugar (¾ cup)
Brown sugar (2 table-
  spoons firmly packed)
Sugar (6 tablespoons)
Cocoa (¼ cup)
Cinnamon (1½ teaspoons)

DO-AHEAD TIMETABLE

Up to a month ahead: Bake and freeze cinnamon rolls

One day ahead: Cut cantaloupe or grapefruit. Prepare fruit. Thaw cinnamon rolls

Just before serving: Heat cinnamon rolls. Blend drink and garnish with strawberry. Fill cantaloupe or grapefruit with prepared fruit

Amaretto Rendezvous

FOR 2 SERVINGS

A smooth and fruity drink flavored with almond liqueur and garnished with a strawberry.

Ice cubes
1½ cups bottled pineapple-coconut juice (preferably without added sugar)
½ cup (4 ounces) Amaretto di Saronno liqueur
2 heart-shaped strawberries, to garnish (optional)

Fill blender container ⅓ full of ice cubes. Add juice and liqueur and blend until ice cubes are dissolved. Pour into stemmed glasses and garnish each glass, if desired, with a strawberry which has been slit at the bottom to hold it onto the rim.

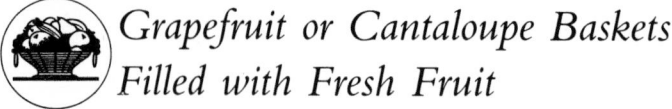

Grapefruit or Cantaloupe Baskets Filled with Fresh Fruit

FOR 2 SERVINGS

1 large grapefruit *or* 1 medium-size ripe cantaloupe
About 2 cups fresh fruit in season, such as orange, melon, fresh berries, kiwi, pomegranate

TO GARNISH:

2 mint sprigs

Cut the grapefruit or cantaloupe in half. Make zig-zag notches all around the circumference using a thin, sharp knife or a special garnishing tool. Remove the grapefruit flesh with a grapefruit knife, leaving some pulp next to the rind. Cut the flesh into sections, removing all membrane. If using cantaloupe, use a melon ball cutter, leaving about ¼ inch of flesh next to the rind. Set aside the grapefruit sections or melon balls and turn the hollowed shells upside down to drain.

Meanwhile, prepare the other fruits in bite-size pieces. Mound the fruit, including the reserved grapefruit or cantaloupe, in the shells. Garnish each serving with a sprig of mint.

To Prepare in Advance: These can be assembled the evening before, wrapped loosely in plastic, and refrigerated until serving time.

Gram's Chocolate Cinnamon Rolls

MAKES 10 ROLLS

Paul's mother, Marge, made these very tender rolls for us one Christmas morning and they've been a family favorite ever since. They are easy to make, as the dough requires no kneading.

	Shortening to grease pan
1	package active dry yeast
¾	cup warm water (105 to 115°F)
¼	cup (½ stick) unsalted butter, melted and cooled slightly
¼	cup sugar
¼	cup cocoa
1	egg
½	teaspoon salt
2¼	cups all-purpose flour

FILLING:

3	tablespoons unsalted butter, at room temperature
2	tablespoons firmly packed brown sugar
1½	teaspoons cinnamon
½	cup miniature chocolate chips
⅓	cup chopped walnuts *or* pecans

193

TO DECORATE:

2   tablespoons (¼ stick) butter, at room temperature
¾   cup powdered sugar
    Cream *or* milk
    Chopped pecans *or* walnuts

Grease a 9-inch round pan. Stir the yeast into the warm water until dissolved. Set aside.

In large bowl of electric mixer beat together the melted butter, sugar, cocoa, egg, salt, and 1 cup of the flour until well mixed. Stir in the yeast mixture and continue beating for about 2 minutes at medium speed. Stir in the remaining flour with a wooden spoon. Form into a ball, cover with a damp towel, and let rise in a warm spot for about an hour, or until doubled in bulk.

Punch the dough down and place on buttered foil. Roll into a 12 x 9-inch rectangle.

For the filling, spread 3 tablespoons softened butter over the dough. Sprinkle with brown sugar, cinnamon, chocolate chips, and ⅓ cup chopped nuts. Roll up lengthwise. Cut into 10 equal slices and arrange, cut side down and sides touching, in prepared pan. Again cover with a damp towel and allow to rise in a warm place for about 30 minutes, or until doubled in size. Meanwhile, preheat oven to 375°F. Bake rolls for 25 minutes, or until lightly browned. Remove from oven and spread tops with 2 tablespoons soft butter. Combine powdered sugar and enough cream or milk to make a glaze and spread over the rolls. Sprinkle with nuts.

Serve warm.

To Prepare in Advance: Freeze rolls after baking and glazing. Warm, covered with foil, in a 300°F oven for 20 to 30 minutes.

INDEX

INDEX

197